D1547386

HOLDING AND LETTING GO

HOLDING AND LETTING GO

The Social Practice of Personal Identities

Hilde Lindemann

OXFORD
UNIVERSITY PRESS

OXFORD
UNIVERSITY PRESS

Oxford University Press is a department of the University of Oxford.
It furthers the University's objective of excellence in research, scholarship,
and education by publishing worldwide.

Oxford   New York

Auckland   Cape Town   Dar es Salaam   Hong Kong   Karachi
Kuala Lumpur   Madrid   Melbourne   Mexico City   Nairobi
New Delhi   Shanghai   Taipei   Toronto

With offices in

Argentina   Austria   Brazil   Chile   Czech Republic   France   Greece
Guatemala   Hungary   Italy   Japan   Poland   Portugal   Singapore
South Korea   Switzerland   Thailand   Turkey   Ukraine   Vietnam

Oxford is a registered trademark of Oxford University Press
in the UK and certain other countries.

Published in the United States of America by
Oxford University Press
198 Madison Avenue, New York, NY 10016

Library of Congress Cataloging-in-Publication Data
Lindemann, Hilde.
Holding and letting go : the social practice of personal identities / Hilde Lindemann.
pages cm
Includes bibliographical references and index.
ISBN 978-0-19-975492-2 (hardcover : alk. paper)
1. Identity (Psychology)—Social aspects.   I. Title.
BF697.L53555 2014
155.9'2—dc23
2013018076

1 3 5 7 9 8 6 4 2
Printed in the United States of America
on acid-free paper

This book is for Paul.

CONTENTS

PREFACE

Holding and Letting Go is a work in philosophy that aims to describe a moral practice we engage in constantly, but that has not received much recognition *as* a moral practice: it is the practice of initiating human beings into personhood and then holding them there. I argue that personhood consists of four elements: (1) a human being has sufficient mental activity to constitute a personality, (2) aspects of this personality are expressed bodily, (3) other persons recognize it as the expression of a personality, and (4) they respond to what they see. Recognition and response are often a matter of understanding who someone is and treating them accordingly. Whether these understandings are self-conceptions or others' sense of who we are, they consist of a web of stories depicting our most important acts, experiences, characteristics, roles, relationships, and commitments. This narrative tissue constitutes our personal identities, which play a crucial role in the practice of personhood.

Our personal identities fuel the practice because they indicate who we are with respect to other persons and in that way guide not only how we are supposed to treat those others but also how we are supposed to conduct ourselves. As the practice of personhood is governed by rules that are both socially and morally normative, my description of how we engage in the practice aims to capture something important about how morality functions.

We are initiated into personhood though interactions with other persons, and we simultaneously develop and maintain personal identities through interactions with others who hold us in our identities. This holding can be done well or badly. Done well, it supports an individual in the creation and maintenance of a personal identity that allows her to flourish personally and in her interactions with others. Done badly, we hold people in invidious, destructive narratives. Some such narratives identify the social group to which someone belongs as socially and morally inferior, and in that way the stories uphold abusive power relations between "us" and "them." In other cases, we hold people too long in identities that no longer serve them, preventing them from moving on fully to identities that do.

My descriptions of how personhood is practiced display a naturalized moral epistemology. But "naturalized" means different things to different people, so I'll explain what I mean by it here. What all naturalizing moves have in common is a rejection of a priori, idealized judgments that have no connection with actual on-the-ground practices. Annette Baier, for one, has argued that the problems with an idealized moral epistemology are twofold: not only does idealized moral knowledge fail precisely where moral norms cannot be defended in actual practice, but ideal theory's assumptions leave us with guidance that is either too vague to be useful in hard cases or so precisely specific that we would constantly have to wonder about legitimate exceptions (Baier 1985). Like Wittgenstein's wheel that can be turned but is not part of the machinery (Wittgenstein 2001, §271), an idealized moral epistemology seems to have no actual role to play in real-time, here-and-now morality.

Many moral philosophers who endorse a naturalized episte-mology have followed W.V.O. Quine in naturalizing knowledge to scientific knowledge, although as morality has to do with human conduct, they naturalize to the social sciences: anthropology, psy-chology, sociology. In Europe, for example, there is an entire move-ment in bioethics called empirical ethics whose epistemology does just that (Musschenga 2005), while the recent turn to experimental philosophy not only draws on data from social and developmental psychology but also has philosophers design and conduct their own experiments (Knobe and Nichols 2008).

The social sciences can, to be sure, illuminate how people live and how they understand their way of life. But Margaret Urban Walker argues that "much of our understanding of how the world in fact is and could be is available not only through commonsense knowledge, but through refined and methodic inquiries that are not scientific, or are of the more dubiously scientific sorts" (Walker 2003, 174). The humanities and the arts yield helpful moral knowl-edge: historians can show us how morality changes over time; phi-losophy, literary studies, and cultural studies provide resources that help us think critically about distributions of moral responsibilities and the social orders they support. Novelists, poets, playwrights, and other artists can help us see the intricate ways in which moral-ity works out—often painfully—in everyday life or show us how it might change for the better. Biographers can tell us about admi-rable, unsatisfactory, and ordinary lives. Like Walker, I take the goal of moral inquiry to be understanding and employing the norms that are embedded in our best moral thinking, while—like Otto Neurath's mariners, who rebuild their boat at sea—at the same time it continuously reevaluates each norm in the light of the others.

I begin this book with the story of my sister, who was very badly cognitively impaired, because her personhood underscores something specific about persons that philosophers have too frequently overlooked: they are made and maintained through the activity of other persons. But if that is so, it raises all kinds of interesting questions. Must we hold in personhood all those who can be so held? When does that activity start? Who starts it? How do we learn to participate in the practice of personhood, and what else must we learn to be able to do this? What, precisely, is the connection between holding someone in personhood and holding her in a particular identity? How do we typically hold each other in various aspects of our identities, and what is usually involved in letting some parts of an identity go? How does this holding go wrong, and what are some of the moral norms that govern it? What does excellent holding look like? Can groups of people, as well as individuals, be held in their identities? What makes it particularly hard to hold people in their identities?

In the rest of this book, I offer preliminary answers to these questions by developing my account of the practice of personhood and the identity-work—the holding and letting go of various aspects of someone's identity—that lies at the heart of it. I begin where human life begins, at gestation, and I follow the trajectory of a normal human lifespan through childhood, adulthood, old age, terminal illness, and death.

In chapter 2, I describe how human fetuses are called into personhood, and I consider what responsibilities a pregnant woman might have to call to her fetus in this way. I explain why, although fetuses aren't yet persons and the right to abort them must be legally protected, so many women nevertheless feel that they could never have an abortion. I make explicit the connection between the practice of personhood and the practice of identity-work, and I explain why so much identity-work must be done close up, as it were—by intimates rather than strangers.

In chapter 3, I consider the process of identity formation, which, from the parents', siblings', and other caregivers' perspectives, is a complex procedure of holding and letting go of the various stories that depict and then no longer depict the child's rapidly changing self. Drawing on John McDowell's notion of "second nature" (McDowell 1996), I show how children are initiated into the practice of personhood as they acquire their second natures, and I connect this initiation to the child's moral formation. I describe how the social kinds to which we belong enter into our identities. Finally, I consider how children's rapidly changing identities can be damaged and why children especially need to be held in their identities when this sort of damage threatens them.

In chapter 4, I describe what is involved in expressing and maintaining already-formed identities under normal circumstances. I liken one's self-comportment in an ordinary social interaction to a theatrical improvisation, in which all the actors project facets of their identities that require uptake from the others on stage if the scene is to go smoothly. I then look at some of the many ways in which these improvisations can go wrong, using the four elements of personhood enumerated earlier as a framework for the ethical analysis. I revisit the question of whether we must ordinarily hold each other in personhood and explain what admirable, poorly executed, and clumsy holding look like.

In chapter 5, I turn away from the paradigmatically mutual forms of holding and letting go that take place among morally competent adults to take a closer look at the ethics of more demanding forms of holding. Catastrophic changes in people's lives that drastically alter their identities can leave others struggling to catch up, as can radical conversions; here in particular, we can be puzzled about what counts as good-enough holding and appropriate letting go. I then take up the problem of socially impossible identities, the ethics of holding or letting go of hypocrites' and wantons' identities, and how best to respond to those whose identities lie at the limits of responsibility, where there is no settled, socially shared moral understanding of what we may or must do for them. I end the chapter by once more revisiting the duty to hold someone in personhood, this time examining whether the duty persists even when someone has irrevocably lost her second nature.

Chapter 6 takes up the question of holding and letting go at the end of life and after death. In it, I consider how proxy decision makers hold dying patients in their identities and why contemporary medical practice makes this particularly difficult. Then I look at the disagreements that arise among family members each trying to hold the dying in their own way. After that, I explore how the dying hold the living in their identities and how, even here, that kind of holding can misfire. And finally I note the identity-work that goes on, for better or worse, after someone has died: both how the dead hold the living in various ways and the acts of preservative love by which the living hold the dead.

In chapter 7, which is really more of a coda, I invite the reader to step back and reflect on the point of the practice of personhood: to make human interaction, and therefore society, possible. I provide a general summary of what the book's many depictions of holding and letting go reveal about the role of personal identities in our moral lives and note some of the gaps in my account that still need to be filled in. And finally, I explain why the picture of persons I've created might be particularly helpful here and now, in the contemporary United States.

Readers who come to accept this picture are well positioned to see morality as an ongoing interpersonal exchange, something like a conversation (McKenna 2012) in which expression and uptake centrally involve the narrative tissues that constitute our identities.

That is so because the societies in which identities are constructed and maintained are shot through with morality: to participate in personhood is to participate in moral life. I don't so much argue for this thesis, though, as show the willing where to look and, perhaps more important, how to recognize what's there to be seen. That's the naturalizing move—*denk nicht, sondern schau*. It's when we pay attention to what we actually do with our identities that we discover a neglected but fascinating dimension of morality, just waiting to be explored.

ACKNOWLEDGMENTS

I began my work on what turned out to be this book with an idea I didn't understand very well, and it has taken me ten years to achieve even my current imperfect grasp of what, for lack of a better word, I call "holding." The articles I wrote on the topic over that span of time now serve as the basis of many of the chapters, although all have been considerably reworked. The core of chapter 1 is "What Child Is This?" *Hastings Center Report* 32, no. 6 (2002): 29–38. Chapter 2 contains portions of "The Architect and the Bee: Some Reflections on Postmortem Pregnancy," *Bioethics* 8, no. 3 (1994): 247–67 and " 'But *I* Could Never Have One': The Abortion Intuition and Moral Luck," Special Issue in Honor of Claudia Card, *Hypatia* 24, no. 1 (Winter 2009): 41–55. Chapter 5 owes something to "On the Mend: Alzheimer's and Family Caregiving," *Journal of Clinical Ethics* 16, no. 4 (2005): 307–13. Chapter 6 contains large portions of "Holding on to Edmund: The Relational Work of Identity," in *Naturalized Bioethics: Toward Responsible Knowing and Practice*, ed. Hilde Lindemann, Marian Verkerk, and Margaret Urban Walker (New York: Cambridge University Press, 2009). I'm beholden to

Michigan State University, whose HARP grant provided the course release that allowed me to finish the book, and to the members of the MSU Philosophy Department, who have been unfailingly supportive.

Many people helped me to develop the ideas I've worked out here. I am deeply in debt to my dear friend Sara Ruddick, with whom I had long conversations about holding—and many other things—and who firmly believed in the project of the book. Marian Verkerk has been another wonderful thinking partner, as well as a coauthor and close friend. Cora Diamond's early encouragement was extremely helpful, as were the generous comments of my OUP referees. Margaret Olivia Little offered insightful suggestions for chapter 1, Elise Robinson explained to me what I was trying to say in chapter 2, Ásta Sveinsdóttir generously read and commented on an earlier version of chapter 3, Ellen Chemay gave me valuable advice about chapter 4, members of the Consortium on the Ethics of Families in Health and Social Care pushed me to think harder about some of the identities in chapter 5, and Claudia Card showed me what to do when I got my metaphoric shoelaces in a knot in chapter 6. Rebecca Kukla reminded me that people sometimes need to be prodded into letting go of certain aspects of their identities; Eva Feder Kittay prompted me to deepen my understanding of the normative dimensions of holding for the "Cognitive Disability: A Challenge to Moral Philosophy" conference held in New York, in September 2008; Grant Gillet invited me to consider coercive holding for the Philosophy, Psychiatry and Psychology Conference held at Queenstown, New Zealand, in July 2009; and Lars-Christer Hydén very kindly asked me to give a talk about second nature at the workshop "Dementia, Identity, Personhood," held at Linköping University, Sweden, in September 2010. I owe grateful thanks to them all.

My deepest gratitude, however, goes to my sometime coauthor, best friend, and most loving partner, James Lindemann Nelson, who has, as usual, given me brilliantly insightful comments and suggestions for nearly every chapter of this book, as well as working out with me, over the course of years of conversation, many of its central ideas. He is, hands down, the most creative philosopher I've ever known, and it's been my great good fortune to have worked so closely with him over the last quarter of a century or so. Finally, I mustn't forget Buddy, my daily canine companion these last few months as the writing went into the home stretch.

HOLDING AND LETTING GO

Chapter 1

What Child Is This?

The Practice of Personhood

Supported by love, any tissue-paper identity may stand like stone.

—Janet Frame

It is a Sunday afternoon in late summer, shortly after my sixth birthday. Downstairs, my mother is entertaining a visitor; the sound of their voices drifts up through the open window. I am alone in the room I share with my brother and sister, and the paper dolls I've been playing with aren't fun anymore. I chew on the end of my long dark braid, forgetting that my mama told me not to. I'm tired of my book, and I don't feel like coloring. I have run out of things to do.

I walk quietly down the hallway and enter my mama and papa's bedroom, a dim and ordered space where the shades have been drawn against the heat. The crib stands at the foot of the bed. Through the wooden bars, I see that Carla's eyes are open, so I speak to her. She stares at me solemnly, and I think that if she could, she would reach for me. The curls feathering her head are damp with sweat and her little undershirt is rumpled, so I carefully lower the rail and slide my arm under her back, lifting her off the mattress.

Holding her horizontal, I slowly carry her from the room, turning sideways as I take her through the door. When we reach the staircase at the end of the hall, I grope with my foot for the step. I keep my eyes on her face, and she returns the gaze, seemingly intent on what I murmur to her as we make our descent. Here is where the stairs turn, so we have to be extra careful. We'll stay close to the wall, and my foot will tell me where the next step is. You're not so heavy, are you, my baby? You want your mama, don't you.... It's pretty dark in here, but we'll be in the kitchen soon. Another step, and then another.

My sandal touches the linoleum at the foot of the stairs. The murmur of voices is louder now, punctuated by my mother's laughter. Again I turn sideways to maneuver us through the doors, and we pass through the empty kitchen and my mama's pretty dining room, where the chocolate brown walls are covered with roses. As we appear in the archway to the living room, my mother sees us and stiffens, breaking off in mid-sentence, coffee cup lowered halfway to the saucer. Then she sets the cup down, forcing her round comfortable face to soften into a smile. "Oh, was Carla awake? Aren't you a good big sister to bring her downstairs. Now come to me slowly. Hold on tight. Be very careful—that's right." As soon as I am in range, she scoops the baby out of my arms and cradles her protectively. She smiles still, but I know I have done something wrong.

In the 1950s, not much could be done about hydrocephaly, a neural tube disorder in which spinal fluid builds up in the brain, exerting pressure that interferes with cerebral function. The intracranial pressure caused by Carla's hydrocephaly was so severe that she couldn't lift her head, turn over, sit up, speak, or grasp objects. I don't remember that she ever smiled. She lacked the ability to swallow and had to be fed through a nasogastric tube that my mother learned how to manipulate at home. Carla's appearance could deceive a casual observer into thinking she was much like any other baby, though a closer look revealed that her head was somewhat larger than normal. She had the translucent complexion that so often accompanies red hair and a remarkably fine pair of blue eyes. I believed she was beautiful, and a look at the snapshots that have survived gives me no reason to change my opinion. Her physicians predicted that she would live for many years, warning that once she grew past infancy, it would be too difficult for my mother to care for her and she would need to be institutionalized. It never came to that. When she was eighteen months old, the part of the brain that regulated her body temperature succumbed to the pressure and ceased to function. In May 1954, two months before my seventh birthday, Carla died of a high fever.

With Carla firmly in mind, I begin my examination of how personal identities function by exploring a one-sided practice that often takes place in families and other structures of intimacy where there is a responsibility to care for someone who is seriously ill or disabled. It is the practice of holding the individual in personhood by constructing or maintaining an identity for her when she cannot, or can no longer, do it for herself. I then want to press four questions. First, how can we make sense of the notion of conferring a personal identity on someone who can contribute nothing to her own personhood? Second, if human beings can be brought into or held in being by how they are treated, then why can't we unilaterally call into personhood just any valued entity? Third, what do we owe to those we hold in personhood? And fourth, must we hold in personhood any being who can be so held?

THE NARRATIVE CONSTRUCTION OF IDENTITIES

Let me begin by explaining what I mean by "maintaining a personal identity." Marya Schechtman has usefully distinguished between two senses of identity. The first has to do with the question of whether a person at one point in time is still the same as the person at an earlier point in time. Call this the reidentification question. The second has to do with how the person sees herself and who other people understand her to be. In this sense of personal identity, the question isn't "Am I still the same person?" but "Who am I?" Call this the characterization question (Schechtman 1996).

I have argued elsewhere (Nelson 2001) that personal identities in the sense of the characterization question are narratively constituted. They consist of tissues of stories and fragments of stories, generated from both first- and third-person perspectives, that cluster around what we take to be our own or others' most important acts, experiences, characteristics, roles, relationships, and commitments: these stories display the various facets of who the person is. They are, that is to say, narrative understandings formed out of the interaction between one's self-concept and others' sense of us. And because stories depict time passing, the narratives that constitute identities can reflect the respects in which we change, as well as how we remain the same.[1]

Many of the narrative understandings forming a part of a personal identity draw on stock plots and character types that are familiar to us all. At some point in your life, perhaps, you might have

---

1. For a recent theory of the narrative nature of identities that responds to criticisms in the philosophical literature but does not take their social construction and maintenance into account, see Davenport 2012.

understood your relationship with a lover by configuring it according to the stock boy-meets-girl script that structures everything from "Cinderella" to Valentine's Day; the story then becomes a piece of your identity-constituting autobiography. A friend betrays you, and you identify him in biblical terms: he is a Judas. A white police officer sees a black teenager driving his mother's BMW and pigeonholes him as a drug dealer or a car thief, drawing on the representations of African American youths that saturate the media. Socially shared narratives like these contribute to the identities of groups as well as individuals, and members of the group draw a part of their identity from how the group identity is narratively constructed.[2]

Other parts of the narrative tissue that constitute a personal identity consist of the localized, particular stories that pick an individual out as distinct from others in the groups to which she belongs: these are the stories that distinguish Carla from the other members of her family or from the class of badly damaged babies in general. They are the stories of Carla's birth and her repeated hospitalizations, of the day my sister bathed her under close maternal supervision, of the time when my father took her outside to show her our tree fort, and of the afternoon I just recounted, when I carried her down the stairs.

Personal identities function as counters in our social transactions, in that they convey understandings of what those who bear them are expected to do. If an answer to "Who are you?" is "the bartender," for example, I expect you to know how to mix a martini;

---

2. According to Anthony Appiah, a collective identity consists of a label picking out a group, the internalization of the label as a part of the identity of at least some individual group members, and the existence of patterns of behavior toward those to whom the label applies (Appiah 2007, 66–69). While I agree with Appiah that the consensus on how to identify those bearing the label is organized around narratives, I do not think the internalization of the label is a necessary part of the identity; others will treat you as a member of the group whether you see yourself as a member or not.

if the answer is "a practicing Muslim," I don't. Moreover, identities also convey understandings of how those who bear them may be treated. If you're my three-year-old son, I can remind you to use the toilet, but if you're my boss, I'd better not. Personal identities thus make intelligible not only how other people are supposed to act, but how *we* are supposed to act with respect to them.

From a first-person perspective, personal identities function in much the same way. I treat myself with contempt or respect depending on who I think I am, and out of that narratively constructed sense of myself, I also establish certain expectations for how I ought to behave in the future. But the fit between my identity and my agency goes in both directions: if it's true that I act out of the tissue of stories that constitute my sense of who I am, it's just as true that I express who I am by how I act. In fact, my actions are important criteria for assessing the accuracy of my self-conception. If, for instance, I see myself as a good driver but I've received four traffic citations in the last six months, others have reason to doubt, in this respect, at any rate, that my identity-constituting stories are credible ones.

As the good driver example reveals, personal identities may be sites of contestation. This is particularly true for members of minority groups who have been persistently misidentified by those in the dominant culture. So, for example, the black teenager driving his mother's BMW doesn't at all view himself the way the white cop does. In his case, the difference of opinion over who he is might, with difficulty, be resolved as soon as his mother comes down to the station house to set the officer straight. In other cases, recognition of a self-understanding may be impossible to come by because the person lacks the social standing that permits her own story about who she is to be taken up by others (Fricker 2009).

THE ROLE OF THE FAMILY

Identity formation begins in infancy and often even earlier, as family members prepare for the birth by folding their newest addition into the ongoing narrative of the life they live in common (I'll have much more to say about this in the next chapter). In the case of a normal, healthy child, the process continues through the child's interaction with the other members of the family. The family therapist Salvador Minuchin puts it this way:

Human experience of identity has two elements: a sense of belonging and a sense of being separate. The laboratory in which these ingredients are mixed and dispensed is the family, the matrix of identity.

In the early process of socialization, families mold and program the child's behavior and sense of identity. The sense of belonging comes with an accommodation on the child's part to the family groups and with his assumption of transactional patterns in the family structure that are consistent throughout different life events. Tommy Wagner is a Wagner, and throughout his life he will be the son of Emily and Mark....

The sense of separateness and individuation occurs through participation in different family subsystems in different family contexts, as well as through participation in extrafamilial groups. As the child and the family grow together, the accommodation of the family to the child's needs delimits areas of autonomy that he experiences as separateness. A psychological and transactional territory is carved out for that particular child. Being Tom is different from being a Wagner. (Minuchin 1974, 47–48)

Tommy *becomes* who he is through a mutual process of accommodating himself to his family and being accommodated by it—and though Minuchin doesn't say much about this, the process profoundly affects the identities of the other family members as well. Moreover, by interacting with his family, Tommy also *expresses* who he is. Because Tommy is a child, he expresses himself clumsily, of course. But his actions do reveal some things about him. They exhibit his likes and dislikes, who and what he cares about, whether he is fearful or foolhardy, affectionate or reserved. It's the stories that he and his family construct around his acts, and around the other things about Tommy that matter most to them, that form Tommy's identity. Because Tommy can speak and act, he collaborates in the construction of his identity. He contributes first-person stories to the narrative tissue that represents who he is.

THE NARRATIVE CONSTRUCTION OF CARLA'S IDENTITY

Now let's return to Carla. It's doubtful that she was capable of forming a self-conception, and even if she did have some sense of who she was, she certainly lacked the ability to express it. The narrative tissue that constituted her personal identity therefore contained no stories from her own, first-person perspective. It was constructed entirely from the third-person point of view. We who were her family, along with friends, neighbors, and the many health care professionals she encountered in her short life, gave her all the identity she had.

Could we have misidentified her? Of course we could. Though Carla couldn't, by word or deed, contest our narratives of who she was, there were a number of other constraints on the credibility of our stories. For one thing, there was the limit imposed by her disability. If my father had, for instance, constructed out of equal parts of hope and grief a story about Carla's being just a bit slower to develop than we older children were, the story would not have been a credible contribution to her identity. Had my four-year-old brother, acting out of his narrative understanding of her, demanded that she play trains with him, his narratives would have had to be judged defective as well. Nor was her disability the only constraint on the accuracy of our stories. Her neurologist couldn't credibly set her within the identity-constituting narratives of the family down the street. I couldn't credibly represent her as my older sister. No personal identity is infinitely malleable; all are bound by facts of one kind or another.

If, however, there are a number of ways for the stories that constitute an identity to go wrong, there are also a number of ways for them to go right. On that Sunday afternoon when I brought Carla down the stairs, my mother's complicated reaction was both an acknowledgment of my good intentions and an indication that she saw Carla primarily as a terribly sick little baby. Her hydrocephaly seems to have been the thing about Carla that mattered most to my mother, and indeed she wove many of her stories of who Carla was around that fact. I, on the other hand, seem to have been too young to appreciate the seriousness of her condition, so while it entered into my narrative conception of her, I saw her primarily as a playmate. I wasn't then a competent judge of how well my playmate story identified her, but as I remember that incident now, I still think the narrative was a credible contribution to Carla's identity.

Each of us in the family, I daresay, saw Carla in a slightly different light. Acting on our various conceptions of who she was, we made a place for her among us, treating her according to how we saw her, and in so treating her, making her into even more of the person we saw. Because I played with her, she was my playmate. Because my mother cared for her at home, she was a member of the household. There were five of us engaged in the narrative work of forming and preserving Carla's identity, and while many of the stories were ones we shared in common, we all added individual bits and pieces of our own. The more we did this, the richer her identity became. All of us, singly and severally, were contributing to what it meant to be Carla. To the extent that our narratives reflected faithfully who she was within our family, even we children, who were not yet full moral agents, were taking part in the creation and maintenance of something morally valuable. We were holding her in personhood.

WAS CARLA A PERSON?

The language of "persons" and "personhood" is perhaps employed more often by philosophers than by less peculiarly educated people. In ordinary conversation, we typically talk, not of persons, but of consumers, stepmothers, pedestrians, and literary critics. Implicit in these terms, however, and common to them all, is the complicated set of reactions and attitudes that both express and sustain what is fundamentally a special moral relationship. The thought that this toddler or that passenger is a person very likely doesn't cross our minds, but assumptions about how they are to be regarded and what we may or must not do to them lie at the heart of our conception of the entities with whom we share our way of being in the world.

My parents, siblings, and I took up these assumptions and attitudes toward Carla, and if you'd asked us whether she was a person, we would have pitied you for being a philosopher and said, "Of course." But it's here that we have to ask the question of how it make sense to construct a personal identity for someone who can contribute nothing to her own personhood. Can we truthfully say that Carla had any personhood for us to acknowledge? Isn't "person" simply an honorific that the rest of us bestowed on her—a kind of "as if" that tugs at the heartstrings but is nonetheless a philosophical confusion (Engelhardt 1975)? Surely, we might object, she wasn't really a person. She didn't, after all, measure up to the ordinary criteria for personhood that have been advanced in the philosophical literature.

She wasn't capable of rational reflection, as required by Immanuel Kant's, John Rawls's, Tamar Shapiro's, and Christine Korsgaard's theories (Kant 1998, Rawls 1971, Shapiro 1999, Korsgaard 2009). She probably wasn't self-aware, which is Michael Tooley's criterion (Tooley 1983). It wasn't clear to what extent we could ascribe intentional predicates to her, as P. F. Strawson would have us do (1959). She wasn't able to treat others as persons, as Rawls (again) and Thomas Nagel specify (Rawls 1971, Nagel 1972). She couldn't communicate with us verbally, as Daniel Dennett says she must (Dennett 1976). She wasn't capable of forming second-order desires, as Harry Frankfurt requires (1988a). She couldn't, as Schechtman would have it, organize her experiences, acts, or relationships into an autobiographical narrative (Schechtman 1996). Notice how all these criteria are based on the individual's own capacities and capabilities—and how, in many cases, they're identical to the criteria for moral agency. By all these measures, Carla flat-out flunked the personhood test.

About all she had going for her was that we treated her in certain ways, and according to Amélie Rorty (1962), Hilary Putnam (1964), Wilfrid Sellars (1966), Antony Flew (1968), Cora Diamond (1991a), and Carl Elliott (2001), our treating her in these ways is somehow and to some extent what makes her a person. But how can this be? Under what circumstances does third-person identity construction confer actual rather than merely honorific personhood?

THE ATTITUDE TOWARD A SOUL

Elliott's account of persons seems to suggest an answer. He begins with Wittgenstein's remark in the *Philosophical Investigations*, "My attitude towards him is an attitude towards a soul. I am not of the *opinion* that he has a soul" (Wittgenstein 2001, 152). Following Wittgenstein, Elliott argues that to treat someone as a person does not involve knowing that "this is a person," but rather consists in taking up a certain attitude or stance toward her. Implicit in this stance is the recognition that the person has certain rights, is properly the object of various moral duties, and so on, and to that extent, we can speak of the attitude toward a soul as a moral attitude. But it's also more than that. It includes taking for granted that persons wear clothes and are given names rather than numbers, and that they are to be referred to as "who" instead of "what." The stance we take toward persons is one we learn, and we learn it so early and so thoroughly that it becomes second nature. Elliot writes, "Our attitudes toward other beings are built into the language that we use to describe them, and the language is embedded in a way of behaving toward them—what Wittgenstein calls a 'practical method.' This practical method is not something that is best described as deliberative action, but something that is reactive and habitual" (Elliott 2001, 97). How we think about and behave toward things of a certain type is tied to the attitude we are taught to take toward such things, and this in turn is tied to the form of life we inhabit.

The form of life is important, Elliott contends, because the biological characteristics to which the concept of personhood is connected (such as the capacity for speech) become significant when cultures make something of them, and different cultures understand these characteristics differently. Elliott writes, "It would not surprise me, for example, to hear an anthropologist speak about one culture that revered...damaged children and another culture that simply discarded them, and that each attitude was tied in complex and subtle ways to the culture's religion, structures of kinship, beliefs about health and illness, and so on" (Elliott 2001, 98–99). Treating someone as a person involves a range of attitudes, and these differ somewhat from one culture to the next.

Because Elliott's account consists of a description of linguistic practices connected to reaction and habit within a given form of life, it answers the question of how my family's response to Carla makes sense with an empirical consideration: "This is simply what we do." The difficulty with this answer, however, is that it doesn't resolve the question of whether we ought to do it *here*, in this puzzling instance. What we wanted to know was how we should proceed in the outlier cases, where there doesn't seem to be any one settled thing we do. So we need to find another way of making sense of the idea that someone could be held in personhood entirely by others' actions. To do that, we might take a somewhat closer look at what Wittgenstein himself has to say about souls.

EMBODIED PERSONS

In the same section of the *Philosophical Investigations* but farther down the page, Wittgenstein says that "the human body is the best picture of the human soul" (Wittgenstein 2001, 152). All of the section containing this remark deals with how we recognize and respond to people's so-called psychological or mental states—what we tend to think of as people's inner lives. It's people's bodies that express whether they are excited, puzzled, or interested; whether they are amused, fearful, or determined. So, in reading their bodies—their postures, gestures, and expressions—we are simultaneously reading what's "in" their minds. And it's our ability to read human bodies in this way that allows us to see human beings as personalities rather than as furniture, plants, or pets (Walker 1998, 181).

In his explanation of *how* we read bodies, Elliott rightly emphasizes Wittgenstein's insistence that this is something we have had to learn. As Margaret Urban Walker puts it, "We have to grasp the code of recognition (what Wittgenstein called the 'method of projection' or the 'application' of a kind of picture) that connects certain displays with certain meanings, and so makes a picture show what it does" (Walker 1998, 182). But the point here isn't only that this kind of recognition and response requires training—it's that there is something here to be recognized. There is something to get right or wrong, something we can see or misperceive, something to which we can respond well or badly. Your grimace might be a manifestation of chagrin (an expression of personality) that I mistake for an involuntary reflex (an expression of indigestion, perhaps). Or I might register your smile as a smile but fail to recognize that it's an angry smile. Most of us, though, manage fairly successfully most of the time to read other people's psychological or emotional states from the comportment, behavior, or expression of their bodies.

Frequently, this involves attending to a number of bodily movements in a combination that's intelligible only in certain settings and sequences. Then it's the very specificity of the configuration-in-context that lets us zero in on the person's subjectivity, in much the same way as the detail in a map leads us to the particular house we are trying to find. If we share enough of the context and have learned how to look, we can usually tell when someone is feeling triumphant, or gets the joke, or resents the intrusion.

What's there to be recognized (or misunderstood) is the changing procession of sensations, emotions, beliefs, attitudes, wishes, misgivings, and other mental states that cross a human consciousness. The capacity to generate selected items in this procession has been taken by some philosophers to be either necessary or sufficient for personhood, but I want to suggest instead that the psychological states themselves are the stuff around which personhood coalesces. If we take seriously, as I believe we must, that these states are socially mediated and that persons, too, are essentially social, then, rather than tying personhood solely to capabilities and competencies residing within the individual, we have to see it as largely also an interpersonal achievement.

Pushing Wittgenstein's "picture" remark one step further, let me propose that our psychological states, their bodily representations, others' uptake of these representations, and the treatment based on that uptake all play a part in the formation and maintenance of personhood. Put more precisely, my claim is that personhood just *is* the bodily expression of the feelings, thoughts, desires, and intentions that constitute a human personality, as recognized by others, who then respond in certain ways to what they see. *Recognition* includes establishing a personal identity by engaging in the narrative activity that constitutes our sense of who the person is. *Response* includes the attitudes and actions we take toward the person—what we do to or for the person and what we expect from the person—on the basis of that identity-constituting, narrative activity. The bodily depiction of the succession of mental states and its uptake by others in the form of recognition and response make up what can be called the social practice of personhood, the practice on which all other social practices rest.

The tissue of stories that constitute our identities are representations of persons—that is, they portray the individuals who participate in the practice of personhood. But what, exactly, is it they portray? Personhood, on my Wittgensteinian account, is a matter of expression and recognition, of playing roles in a kind of human drama. But in a drama there is a distinction between the character an actor is playing and the actor who plays that character. If identities are analogous to characters, what's the analogue to the actor who brings the character to life on stage? I take it that the analogue is the self, where a self is understood as the locus of idiosyncratic causation, sensation, and experience.[3] This self is socially shaped by the very practices in which it participates, and because selves change over time, the stories that once represented them—if they are to represent them accurately—must fall out of the narrative tissue, to be replaced by newer stories that capture what is important about the self as it is now.

On a Wittgensteinian analysis it makes no sense, in the standard case, to say that we know someone is a person ("I am not of the *opinion* that he has a soul"). Matters are different in the outlier cases. It *does* make sense to ask of someone in a persistent vegetative state, or an anencephalic baby, or someone suffering from the later stages of Alzheimer's disease, whether they are persons. The reason it makes sense is that the further away we move from the paradigm case, the more difficult it is to apply the concept. What complicates the matter further is that the narrative process of identity constitution usually begins before the entity becomes a person, often continues after

---

3. I'm grateful to Naomi Scheman for helping me with this formulation.

the person no longer exists, and sometimes fails altogether because the person for whom the identity is created never does, as it happens, come into being.

The embodied, social account of personhood I'm proposing can help us distinguish among these outlier cases. Carla had experiences and sensations; she could fix her attention; she could be comforted. These mental states were enough, I think, for the family's practice of personhood to get a toehold, even though Carla's own contribution to that practice was severely limited. By the same token, someone who has become progressively more demented may still retain enough cognitive functioning to be held in personhood by her loved ones or by kind and caring professionals. Anencephalics and those in the persistent vegetative state, on the other hand, are incapable of even the minimal psychological activity around which personhood could be formed. Where there are no mental states, there is nothing for the body to express, no picture for others to recognize. In these cases, I am inclined to say that there is no meaningful possibility of bringing into existence, or continuing to maintain, the individual's personhood. The attempt to hold the individual in personhood misfires; the concept of "person" has been misapplied.

On the view I am proposing, fetuses aren't persons either, but for a different reason. Although late-term fetuses, at any rate, typically seem to be capable of sensing, fearing, and wanting, the fact that they are hidden from view makes it impossible for others to engage in the recognition and response that would otherwise bring them into personhood. The one exception is the pregnant woman herself, who can play out the requisite practices of personhood once she feels the fetus move. But her ability to do this is severely circumscribed by the limited pictorial repertoire available to the fetus: a sharp dig of an elbow, a series of kicks, the fluttering sensation produced by movements of the hands or feet—all of which might mean anything, or nothing.

Nevertheless, in a pregnancy, the narrative work of constructing a personal identity often does make sense, even though the work might begin many months before the fetus is brought to term. It makes sense in the cases where the pregnancy is wanted, because then there is an expectation that the fetus will become a born child, and identity construction is a way of anticipating the child's personhood. In other cases, the woman carrying the fetus might refrain from weaving narratives of personal identity around the fetus, because she doesn't want the fetus to become her child. In still other cases, the woman begins the process of identity construction and then either decides she must abort, miscarries, learns that the baby is anencephalic, or undergoes a stillbirth, any of which might occasion the same grief and anguish as the loss of a child. And sometimes it's another member of the family entirely, or a friend, who undertakes the imaginative labor of conferring an anticipatory personal identity on the fetus. Whether the identity is actually the identity of a person depends on the outcome of the pregnancy.

The fetal sonograms that have become such a regular part of a middle-class pregnancy contribute greatly to this process of ⌈anticipatory identity construction⌉ precisely because they offer an image of the body to which others can respond. To be sure, it often takes enormous feats of the imagination to make out the fetus's feet, head, or hands. Despite this, doting relatives have become amazingly adept at configuring the blurred shapes to their own satisfaction. As the technology for viewing fetuses in utero becomes more sophisticated, it may well expand the application of the concept of personhood so that it covers fetuses in ever earlier stages of development—particularly as prenatal care involving routine use of fetal imagery becomes universally available.

THE QUESTION OF LIMITS

If my account of personhood is roughly right, then we have to raise a further question. The way we treated our cat was very much like the way we treated Carla. We considered him a member of the household, we fed him and met his other physical needs, we played with him, we had a narrative understanding of who he was, and when he was sick, we took him to the vet's. Moreover, the cat's capacities and capabilities outstripped Carla's by a long chalk. He could purr when we petted him, demand to be fed or go out, express emotions such as fear or frustration, dart as if demon-possessed through all the rooms in the house. If Carla, capable of nothing more than looking at us, could be brought into personhood by how we treated her, then why couldn't the cat?

As Wittgenstein famously remarks about one species of cat, "If a lion could talk, we could not understand him" (Wittgenstein 2001, 190). The reason we couldn't understand him is that lions inhabit an alien form of life, foreign not only in its practices and customs but also in its embodiment. What a lion sees, smells, and hears; how it keeps its balance; the amount of sleep and freedom of movement it requires; the shape of its mouth and teeth—all these physical characteristics contribute to a way of being in the world that we humans can only begin to comprehend. The obstacle to our comprehension isn't just that lions are wild—it's that they're not human. Even domesticated cats, who live in our houses with us and adapt themselves to our comings and goings, can't be said to share in our form of life. The way of being that is supported by their embodiment is simply too far removed from ours for us to draw cats into our human practices of personhood. Cora Diamond has something like this in mind when she writes:

> We, who share this striking thing—having a human life to lead—may make in imagination something of what it is to have a human life to lead; and this imaginative response we may see (and judge and learn from) in the doings and words and customs of those who share *having a human life to lead*. That perception may belong to the understanding we want of those words or actions or customs. (The actions in which the sense of human life is perceivable include but are by no means limited to actions affecting other living human beings.) (Diamond 1991b, 43–44)

There is something that it is like to share in the distinctively human condition, for all the many great differences among human beings. I don't mean simply that human beings occupy what Wilfred Sellars called "the logical space of reasons" (Sellars 1956, 298–99)—obviously, Carla did no such thing, nor do any of us on first entering that condition. But Carla had a human life to lead, not only because of her human embodiment but also because she was born into the nexus of human relationships that made her one of us. She was my sister, my mother's baby, my Oma's grandchild, my father's daughter, and in that way she was ours as no cat or other kind of animal could ever be.[4]

There are many ways of valuing the nonhuman animals with whom we are in relationship: we can love them, name them, play with them, share living space with them, and teach them. And we certainly have moral responsibilities toward them, many of which

---

4. Thanks to Rita Charon for helping me to get clear on this question.

are the same as our responsibilities to persons. But we can't occupy their lifeworld, nor can we fully bring them into ours.

Humans, it seems, can confer personhood only on other humans. But couldn't Martians or dolphins or angels also participate in something like the practices of personhood that, among humans, take the form of displays by, and responses to, the human body? We can certainly imagine such a possibility, though perhaps only with respect to corporeal beings. (Anyone who has ever read all of *Paradise Lost* will remember the crashingly bad verse Milton produced when he tried to depict angels' bodiless digestive systems. Attempts to imagine their interpersonal relations can, I suspect, only go downhill from there.) The trouble with what we can imagine is that it's so easy to import all sorts of questionable assumptions into our imaginings. Just as we imagine that we could understand a talking lion, so, too, we imagine that incorporeal persons could have something we are familiar with because we recognize it in human beings, but which is completely unrelated to the criteria *by* which we recognize it in human beings.

Other corporeal beings, however, do engage in expressive and responsive behaviors bearing at least some similarity to those that sustain human practices of personhood. Elephants, for example, seem to engage in the distinctive patterns of recognition and response reserved for members of their kind (Bates et al., 2008), and presumably any species of animal that lives in packs, herds, schools, or flocks employs such behaviors. In this book, however, I confine myself to an examination of human personhood and leave it to others to determine how like or unlike it is to what other animals do.

None of my remarks are intended to supply sufficient conditions for personhood. They are meant, rather, to describe a social practice. Like other social practices, this one is normatively binding—I can't just decide that Carla is a table, and I can't just declare that personhood extends to cats—but again like other social practices, it contains critical resources for its own evaluation and revision. We can reflect on what our practice leaves out, argue about whether it includes too much, give reasons for changing certain aspects of the practice or revising our understandings of what it entails. And because personhood is as much a moral as a social concept, we can test, refine, and question our beliefs about what is owed to those who participate in the practice.

HOLDING AND LETTING GO

The account of personhood I am proposing, then, is of a social practice involving four components: a procession of mental states, expression of these states by a human body, recognition of what is expressed, and response on the basis of that recognition. The account allows for the possibility that a personal identity could be constituted from a purely third-person perspective, while at the same time setting reasonable limits on the sorts of entities that can be held in personhood by these means. But more needs to be said about why it matters whether Carla was a person. Given her almost total lack of agency and the enormous burden of care this imposed on my parents, did she really need to be held in personhood? Would it have been morally permissible just to let her go?

Here we need to make some distinctions. There are differences between (1) holding or letting go of someone's personhood, (2) holding or letting go of someone's life, and (3) holding or letting go of some part of a person's identity. I'll have much more to say later on about the morality of each of these, but for now, let me lay out some theoretical tools I'll be using throughout this book and put them to work on a preliminary answer to what we owed—and didn't owe—Carla.

Holding or Letting Go of Someone's Personhood

To think carefully about whether there's a duty to hold human individuals in personhood, we might want to distinguish among duties that are impersonally authoritative and those that are personally authoritative. In the most general terms, personhood gives us our selves: we can't be who we are without the other persons who initially hold us and then maintain us in personhood. Because participation in personhood opens us to the riches of a distinctively human life, I am inclined to say that the duty to value any individual who could be a person in the special way reserved for persons is impersonally authoritative, binding on all of us, no matter who we are. Carla's personhood required, for example, that anyone, whether stranger or family member, see her as what Eva Kittay calls "some mother's child" (Kittay 1998, 23), rather than as merely a thing to be cared for, just as it would have prohibited anyone, had the technology then been available, from killing her for the sole purpose of harvesting her organs for others' use.

We can think of requirements and prohibitions of this sort as falling under the general heading of an impersonally authoritative obligation to treat persons in a manner consonant with their value. Elliott tells of his experience as a third-year medical student, following an intern on ward rounds at the county hospital in Charleston, South Carolina. They passed through the room of an elderly woman "who was," says Elliott, "if not permanently vegetative, very close to it." The intern's instructions to Elliott, he recalls, were roughly this: "She's a plant; you're the gardener; your job is to make sure she is watered" (Elliott 2001, 95). There are a number of reasons that health care practitioners say things like that about their patients— for one thing, black humor can be a way of reducing other people's misery to manageable proportions. All the same, this is no way to talk about a person. It might not *harm* a person who is barely conscious to be treated like a plant, but arguably it *wrongs* her, because it pushes her outside the human community. To be sure, even those who can no longer take even a minimally active part in the practice of personhood, such as the dead or those in the persistent vegetative state, ought not to be subjected to indignities. But that is so primarily because of the intimate causal connection between what they are now and the persons they once were or might have been. The immense moral value of lives like yours and mine spills over, as it were, in forward, backward, and sideways directions on humans who can't, or can no longer, be fully held in personhood (Sumner 1981).[5]

Other responsibilities to persons are role-related, but these, too, are impersonally authoritative. Any father, for example, no matter who he is, has a defeasible responsibility to protect, nurture, and love his child. At this level of obligation, Carla's personhood required that her father hold her in her identity as his daughter, that he care for her more deeply than he cared about the neighbors' children, and that he go to considerable lengths, if need be, to meet her physical and medical needs. It required him to play a primary role in keeping her safe from others' negligence or abuse. It also required him to foster such emotional and familial ties as could be forged between her and her siblings. Moreover, because she was his terribly *impaired* daughter, we would find his love defective if it had not been mingled with pain and sorrow.

Holding or Letting Go of Someone's Life

I've just claimed that the duty to hold in personhood anyone who could be so held is impersonally authoritative. But in the tragic cases

---

5. A variation on Sumner's argument is Nolan 1988, and James Lindemann Nelson suggested a further variation to me.

where a living human being is in such a bad way that she would be better off dead, the right thing to do might be to let go of her life, or even kill her directly. And once she is dead, she can't be held in personhood. So now we address the question as to when, if ever, it's morally permissible or even obligatory to let go of someone's life. To sort this out, we need a little more theory.

Jonathan Dancy argues that the reasons for acting in a given set of circumstances take on a specific moral "shape." That is, they cluster together in a particular way that adds up to "this is wrong," or "this is good to do," or some such moral judgment (Dancy 1993). A reason that in one configuration might count for doing something could, in another configuration, count against doing it, or count neither for nor against. Being helpful, for example, is usually a good reason to act—but not when someone needs your help to steal a car. Inflicting pain is usually bad—but not when your patient needs the operation. And because considerations carry their moral import only holistically, there are no laws that govern how these reasons behave. Instead, Dancy contends, understanding the morality of an action is a matter of skill or wisdom in discerning the overall "shape" of the situation—seeing how the moral considerations add up in the given case.

Moral particularism is widely regarded as controversial. The biggest worry has to do with the claimed absence of lawlike structures to govern how moral reasons behave. Without universal principles, after all, we seem to be left with nothing but one-off judgments: it's wrong to cause pain here, good to break a promise there, you are morally bound to look out the window in Knoxville next Thursday. And if there is no structure to moral theory, how could morality ever be learned? For that matter, how could moral matters even be discussed? As Mark Lance and Margaret Little observe, "A discipline— be it ethics or epistemology—empty of any theoretical or law-like generalizations is a discipline with highly attenuated potential for understanding" (Lance and Little 2004, 437).

There is a second worry as well. Moral particularism's context dependency can issue in moral judgments that leave the emotions struggling to catch up. If my duty to let my daughter's life go silences my reasons to care for her, why, instead of the glow of satisfaction that is said to accompany the performance of a duty, do I feel such deep sorrow and grief?[6] One explanation is that there really are moral principles at work in these cases, and the bad feelings come from the moral pull they continue to exert, even though they have been outweighed by other, more stringent ones. Either that, or my feelings are an irrational hangover from having had the authority of what I now believe to be nonexistent moral principles drummed into me since infancy.

Lance and Little, however, offer what is to my mind a more attractive explanation, one that preserves the contextualist insight of moral particularism but doesn't discard the theoretical generalizations that are crucial for moral explanation and justification. They point to "a kind of generalization that is both genuinely explanatory *and* ineliminably exception-laden," because it *privileges* the conditions under which a moral connection holds (Lance and Little 2004, 441). These conditions are privileged, not in the sense that they are the statistically usual ones (they might or might not be), but in the sense that they enjoy explanatory, conceptual, or justificatory priority over nonprivileged conditions. They are privileged when, for example, children are healthy enough to lead decent lives; in that

---

6. Jonathan Dancy's example has to do with hitting your assailant to make him let go of your daughter, where reasons of prudence silence ethical considerations of how hard you should hit. He says that "any natural or moral repugnance must be fought down," but it's the fact that you can have negative feelings when you've done the right thing that interests me here (Dancy 1993, 51–52).

case, the defeasible generalization "parents should care for their children" holds good. If you ought *not* to care for your child, then, it's precisely because the privileged conditions don't obtain: perhaps the family's capacity for care has been overwhelmed by too many demands on it and too few resources, or perhaps the child's unbearable, untreatable suffering is a definitive reason to stop treatment.

Lance and Little's "defeasibility holism" offers a plausible account of how moral generalizations can be robustly explanatory even though they are, necessarily, riddled with exceptions. Moreover, their account remains genuinely particularistic, as there is no algorithm or lawlike principle for determining when a condition is privileged. But this need not daunt us. "Barring the creation of an exhaustive exceptionless theory of privilege, navigating the world remains at bottom a matter of skill—including now a skill at understanding and recognizing what is deviant and normal, what paradigmatic and emendational, what conceptually prior or central. We must know our way around possibility space in a far richer sense than has previously been appreciated" (Lance and Little 2004, 453).

Defeasibility holism also accounts for the seemingly wayward feelings that accompany some moral judgments. The regret or anguish attendant on doing what we must when moral reasons have switched their normal valence or been silenced altogether can be explained as a kind of grief over the failure of privileged conditions to obtain. It's not simply that the conditions *deviate* from the privileged ones; it's that the actors inhabit a morally *defective* situation. It is a bad-making feature of the circumstances that this child's death would be better for her than the dreadful suffering she endures. Would that Carla had been spared her hydrocephaly.

If all this is right, we can see why there might not be any one definitive answer to the question of whether we were morally required to hold Carla in her life. It's not that there is no right answer in any particular case, but rather that we'd have to know quite a lot more about the specific moral shape of *that* case. The most we can say—and even this may not be quite right—is that when it is morally better to let go of someone who could still be held in her life, something has gone badly wrong with the surrounding conditions: we are in the presence of a terrible tragedy.

Holding or Letting Go of Someone's Identity

Now let's turn to the question of which aspects of Carla's identity, if any, we were bound to hold her in. Because we believed we were obligated to hold her in personhood, the duty to weave identity-constituting stories around the things about Carla that mattered most to us was impersonally authoritative, as those stories were the means by which we held her. Epistemic as well as moral norms required all of us to converge on some of the same stories in the narrative tissue that formed her identity: stories having to do with who her sisters and brother were, for example, or why we lived where we did, or what was making her so ill.

Other stories, however, were discretionary, but they might not have been discretionary for specific people in her life. Here I think we can talk about personally authoritative responsibilities. These are the responsibilities that arise out of what Frankfurt calls volitional necessity: I must behave toward this person in a particular way not only because I can't help it, but because I don't want to help it (Frankfurt 1988b, 87). You, being you, might not be bound in the same way.

At this level of responsibility, my mother had to construct stories about Carla according to her own lights, along the lines of how she understood her relationship to her youngest and most vulnerable child. I, being me, had to do it somewhat differently, making sense of who Carla was in the terms that my six-year-old self knew best. Although Frankfurt denies that very young children are capable of the second-order volition that produces this kind of necessity (Frankfurt 1988a, 16), developmental psychologists have repeatedly demonstrated that children as young as three are capable of endorsing or repudiating their first-order desires (Gopnik 2009, 59), which makes me think I really did hold Carla in her identity as my playmate out of volitional necessity. In any case, as I look back on it now, I think I held her in a way that was authoritative for me.

Because identities survive people's lives, they extend beyond their personhood. Once her family and the other people who cared for her engaged in the narrative work of constructing her identity, the stories by which we represented her will survive as long as any of us remember her. Indeed, they'll outlive even those of us who knew her personally, as long as they are handed down to those who come after us. Later, we'll revisit the question whether holding the dead in their identities is required of the living, but for now let me just say that holding Carla in a number of aspects of her identity—as my sister, my playmate, a sick little girl, my mama's baby, and so on—continues to be personally authoritative for me. But I do it in the ways I find I must, while others who knew her do it either as they must or as they choose. Just as we all saw her slightly differently when she was among us, so we remember her slightly differently now that she is gone. And the means by which we *express* what we remember can also differ. I, for example, write about her here, whereas my brother and sister have never, to my knowledge, remembered her in writing.

It can sometimes be difficult to know how to "go on," as Wittgenstein would say—how to follow the rule for the application of a fuzzy concept. When we bioethicists and other philosophers engage in talk of persons, we are apt to conjure up a picture of persons like us: adult human beings who are competent moral agents and who interact more or less freely with other fully developed moral agents. This is surely a paradigmatic picture, but it doesn't accurately represent all of the different kinds of persons there are. "A main cause of philosophical disease—" remarks Wittgenstein, "an unbalanced diet: one nourishes one's thinking with only one kind of example" (Wittgenstein 2001, §593). This chapter serves, I hope, to show why we need to extend our conception of persons beyond that comfortable example. The old picture leaves too much out. Among other things, it doesn't allow us to explain what families are doing when they hold a badly impaired child in personhood.

In the week after Carla died, my mother described our loss in a letter to her own mother. "We still seek her around every corner, although with time the sense of emptiness will surely vanish. And we are all the richer because we were permitted to have her these eighteen months, as in that time we learned so much from her about love, compassion, and patience." My mother's way of holding Carla in personhood shines through these words.

Chapter 2

The Architect and the Bee

Calling the Fetus into Personhood

A spider carries on operations resembling those of the weaver, and many a human architect is put to shame by the skill with which the bee constructs her cell. But what from the very first distinguishes the most incompetent architect from the best of bees, is that the architect has built a cell in his head before he constructs it in wax.

—Karl Marx

She woke from dreaming into the gray dawn. The high shadowy ceiling looked slightly foreign, as if she had just arrived in a strange country—which, in a way, she had. Everything remained itself, of course, but it was all even more so. The racket of birdsong outside the open window was more urgent, the half-light of the waking world more mysterious, the pulse beating at her throat and wrist more insistent than ever before in her life. Careful not to disturb the slumbering form beside her, she eased out of bed, pulled on her robe, and padded barefoot into the kitchen.

When the coffee was ready, she filled her mug and carried it out to the back stoop. By now, the sky was flushed above the rooftops, and the blossoms on the mimosa overhanging the hard-packed dirt yard were visibly pink. A mourning dove perched on the pickup truck, adding his cello note to the cacophony overhead. The leaves hung perfectly still: it was going to be a hot day.

He would leave her now, she knew that. Whatever else his restless wayward life would hold, it wouldn't hold a child. Not at twenty-one, not likely at forty-one either. His smile when she told him would be slow and sweet, and tonight when she got home from work he would have dinner on the table. But in a week or so, he would quit his job or get fired, and then he would move on, maybe to Atlanta or Memphis, and she would never see him again.

A desperate loneliness seized her, and she put both hands around her cup to warm them. She wouldn't tell him. She'd get rid of the baby so he'd never know and be very, very careful not to get pregnant again, and then maybe after a while, when he felt like moving on, he'd take her with him. Nothing was worth the risk of losing him.

She set her coffee down carefully beside her, propped her elbows on her knees, and rested her chin in her cupped hands. They had told her at Planned Parenthood yesterday that the morsel inside her was no bigger than a blueberry. Yet curled tightly within it were maybe eighty years of a life, rich and full of experiences, belonging to a distinct human being. *Her* human being. Her firstborn child, with its own thoughts and imaginings, its things to do and trouble to get into. Her daughter or son.

No, she mustn't think like that. She could barely even support herself—how could she take care of a newborn baby, too? Her mama had the rest of them to look after, and her girlfriends wouldn't want a baby around. She couldn't do it. She didn't know how. Oh God, don't let him leave.

A tiny breeze, carrying with it the smell of garbage from the other side of the fence, lifted the hem of her thin cotton robe. The baby would have fat little feet and dimpled fingers and a mouth shaped like a Cheerio. It would learn how to walk, staggering across the floor and sitting suddenly on its bottom with a bump. Later, he would bang the door when he went outside to play and leave his room in a mess. Or it would be a little girl who would giggle with her at the movies and want her toenails painted. There would be fights and late nights where she would be frantic because she didn't know where he was, and the next day he would waltz her around the kitchen and she would laugh for the sheer joy of him.

She thought of lying on a table with her feet up in stirrups so the doctor could reach inside her to scrape him out. Would God punish her if she did it? No—having an abortion wasn't the same as killing a baby or anything. Lots of women had them because they didn't want to be pregnant right then or maybe ever. It wasn't right to judge them. The doctor would wear a white mask and latex gloves, and there would be a hot bright light overhead and a green sheet that kept her from seeing what he was doing, but she'd feel the sharp knife go in and its tip would find the little blueberry and—. She stopped. She could never have one. No matter what happened. He would leave her and she was terrified and nothing would ever be the same again, but she had a little blueberry now and she would have to take care of it.

Slowly she put her hand on her belly, a gentle anxious figure sitting quietly on the stoop. Out on the street a car door slammed and an engine turned over as the world spun gravely around to meet the dazzling heat of the morning.

THE ABORTION INTUITION

Of the many intuitions people have about abortion, there is one— for present purposes, I'll just call it the abortion intuition—that has received little attention from philosophers, even though many women share it. "It's not wrong to have an abortion," a friend or neighbor or student will say. "I think they should be legal, but *I* could never have one."

On its face, this is a peculiar statement. If abortion is acceptable for everyone else, why should it be wrong for me? Why would I give my moral approval to all abortions except my own? One explanation for the tension created when a person exempts herself like this from what others may do is that she is suffering from a kind of patriarchal hangover: she is liberated enough to see that other women need the freedom to refuse an unwanted pregnancy, but her consciousness is still sufficiently infiltrated by sexist views of women's place in society to make that option seem immoral for her. I think this explanation is too quick, not to mention disrespectful of a great number of women. My own view is that, far from being an epiphenomenon of patriarchy, the abortion intuition arises from a set of genuine moral considerations that ought to be taken seriously.

In this chapter, I mine the intuition for what it can teach us about what we are undertaking when we undertake a pregnancy and what we are stopping when we stop one. I'll argue that the abortion intuition points to something important about human pregnancies that is not generally identified as such: they trigger a complex social apparatus that performs the morally valuable function I conceptualize as calling the fetus into personhood. The primary person calling to the fetus is the pregnant woman herself, but I'll show how her society plays a role in calling to the fetus as well. Finally, I'll explain how identities operate in the practice of personhood and why the protoidentities that fetuses bear are inadequate, in and of themselves, to support the practice.

THE VALUE OF A PREGNANCY

To start the argument that the abortion intuition has something to teach us about pregnancy, let's return to the thought, embedded in the intuition, that pregnancies are valuable. As a way of unpacking that thought, I'll consider two sources of value: the fetus and the pregnant woman's activity. I'll begin with the fetus.

Liminal Persons

Many people, myself included, are inclined to say that although a fetus is not the same as a child—indeed, the question for a woman who contemplates aborting her fetus is precisely whether to allow it to *become* a child—fetuses aren't totally worthless, either. And nor, for that matter, are the embryos from which they grow. In the bioethics literature over the last quarter of a century, this valuation has often been expressed in the language of respect. For example, in 1979 the Ethics Advisory Board of what was then the Department of Health, Education, and Welfare declared that fetuses are "entitled to profound respect"—though not profound enough to refrain from killing them, it seems, since the advisory board declared that fetal tissue could be used in research. The National Institutes of Health's Human Embryo Research Panel concluded in 1994 that the embryo deserved "special respect" as a developing form of human life and justified its recommended restrictions on embryo research on those grounds. The National Bioethics Advisory Commission's 1999 *Ethical Issues in Human Stem Cell Research* also speaks of the respect due to embryos as a form of human life, though it defends the destruction of embryos for the purpose of harvesting the stem cells inside them.

As these conflicting conclusions demonstrate, the language of respect doesn't tell us very much. It gives little guidance for how embryos and fetuses should be treated,[1] and it offers no clues as to what exactly is so respectworthy about things of this kind. To

---

1. "Respect" has licensed limiting stem cell research to a narrow window early in embryonic development, or to embryos only from certain sources, but it hasn't stopped fertility clinics from destroying leftover embryos.

answer these questions, I think we have to look to the paradigmatic persons whom, under the right conditions, with the right kind of help from the gestating woman and the right kind of luck, embryos will become if all goes well.

That paradigmatic persons (waitresses, for example, or unconscious violinists) are enormously valuable is not seriously in doubt. Whether they derive this value—a worth so great that Kant declared it "beyond price"—from their ability to reason or their capacity for rich and various experiences, or whether their worth is basic, not dependent on the value of some other characteristic, need not concern us at the moment. More to the point is how strange it would be if entities of such enormous obvious worth should develop from beginnings worth nothing at all.

The continuum of development between human embryos and mature human beings gives us a reason to value the one if we value the other, although we needn't value them to the same degree. I want to take this observation a step further, to suggest that the worth of a paradigmatic person infuses, to some lesser degree, both the fetus from which the person came and the corpse that is its final state. We treat dead bodies ceremoniously to acknowledge the worth of the people they once were; we construct personalities and futures around growing fetuses to mark the worth of the people they will soon be. The more closely either kind of liminal person approximates paradigmatic persons, the greater its value. That would explain why we don't typically mourn the passing of an embryo that has sloughed off a woman's body instead of attaching itself to the uterine wall—and why we usually *do* mourn a miscarriage in the seventh month of gestation, even if the woman didn't want that particular fetus to become her daughter or son.

If this is right, then we already have a way of understanding what is valuable about a pregnant woman's activity: she is moving a fetus ever closer to paradigmatic personhood. Note, however, that unlike the acorn that grows into an oak unassisted by other trees, fetuses don't just grow into persons by themselves. They are the kinds of things whose value resides in their ability to *become* persons, but it takes a woman to *get* them there. Pregnancy, then, isn't merely something that happens to a woman—it's something she does. It's misleading to think of pregnant women's bodies as flowerpots, ovens, or incubators, because when we do that, we lose sight of how pregnancy requires the exercise of a woman's moral *agency*.

The Architect and the Bee

Amniocentesis, sonograms, fetal surgery, and all the wide panoply of useful and lifesaving obstetrical resources at our disposal have inadvertently underscored a nearly universal belief that pregnancy in human beings is a purely biological process, involving a complex interplay of the woman's bodily mechanisms but requiring nothing further of her except that she not interfere with them. To apply Marx's famous distinction between the architect and the bee (Marx 1930, 169–70), the woman's activity of being pregnant is thought to follow its own preordained patterns. Like the bee, on this common view, the pregnant woman cannot help what she is doing.

This picture is false. Its persistence both testifies to and reinforces social attitudes toward women that are demeaning. Human pregnancy is no more purely biological than any other human activity, which is to say that in important ways, the pregnant woman more nearly resembles the architect than the bee. As is typical for her species, the pregnant woman both obeys the laws of nature and improves on them, ordering and shaping what she finds in the natural world through her own intentional, creative activity. She transforms many natural processes not only by giving thought and care to how she performs them but also by valuing them in certain ways or by infusing them with meaning. Out of the ordinary phenomenon of hunger, for example, she creates a dinner party: she turns the need for food into an occasion for expressing love, celebrating friendship, exercising imagination, or furthering her social ambitions. Like the architect's, her constructions are purposeful and deliberate.

We can see this creativity clearly enough in the difference between how humans build their homes and how bees do it. It's harder to see in the case of pregnancy, but gestation, too, when it's human, is routinely transformed by purposeful activity. For starters, women, unlike other animals, are often pregnant for a *reason*: they may conceive and carry a fetus because they want a special relationship that will last over time, or they want an existing child to have a sibling, or without children they would feel less firmly rooted in the world, or they hope the baby's bone marrow will be a lifesaving match for a dying family member.

Note that many of these reasons treat the baby-to-be as a means to someone else's ends, rather than regarding it solely as an end in itself. Especially when parents undertake a pregnancy for the express purpose of producing a child who can provide lifesaving biomaterial for an older sibling, they can find themselves the targets of a certain amount of moral tut-tutting for using their baby instrumentally. This is understandable enough, when we consider how easy it is to think of the child-to-be as already existing, with its own personality, preferences, and rights: we imagine it as requiring to be loved for its own sake and not for its potential usefulness to others. But the parents' intending to make use of it, even if that is their sole motivation for conceiving it, doesn't by itself warrant moral censure. Whether they do something wrong by what they intend depends entirely on how they treat the child after it's born. If they love it, keep it safe, nurture it, and teach it, they aren't using it solely as a means to another's ends. The bone marrow or cord blood the parents require of it can be seen as an unusual sacrifice, to be sure, but one that falls well within the range of what any of us can reasonably be expected to do for a close family member.

Once having conceived, the purposefulness continues: the woman, like the one with which this chapter began, creates or refuses what is, at bottom, the most deeply intimate relationship a human being can have. To be pregnant, of course (though it's surprising how many discussions in the abortion literature miss this), is to be *occupied*, by an entity that is both you and not you and that makes use of your heart, liver, lungs, other organs, blood, hormones, enzymes, and metabolism for its survival. And just as it makes use of your body, so, too, it makes itself felt in and on that body, changing its contours and the coloration of some of its parts; shifting the organs as it grows to make room for itself; producing nausea, weight gain, euphoria, and varicose veins; and sometimes causing life-threatening conditions such as diabetes, high blood pressure, and preeclampsia. To gestate, then, as Margaret Olivia Little puts it, is to engage in "a particular, and particularly thoroughgoing, kind of physical intertwinement" (Little 1999, 296).

The Legality of Abortion

Must women accept this intertwinement? There is increasing pressure in the United States to force them to do so. According to the Guttmacher Institute,

> The current make up of the U.S. Supreme Court have led some state policymakers to consider the possibility that *Roe v. Wade* could be overturned and regulation of abortion returned to the states. Some state legislatures are considering banning abortion under all or virtually all circumstances; these measures are widely viewed as an attempt to provoke a legal challenge

to *Roe*, while other states are considering abortion bans that would go into effect in the event that *Roe* is overturned. And a number of states still have pre-1973 abortion bans on the books—several of which, in theory, could be enforced if *Roe* were ever overturned. Still other states have laws declaring the state's intent to ban abortion to the extent permitted by the U.S. Constitution....

- 20 states have laws that could be used to restrict the legal status of abortion.
- 4 states have laws that automatically ban abortion if *Roe* were to be overturned.
- 13 states retain their unenforced, pre-*Roe* abortion bans.
- 7 states have laws that express their intent to restrict the right to legal abortion to the maximum extent permitted by the U.S. Supreme Court in the absence of *Roe*. (Guttmacher Institute 2013)

Significantly, what antiabortion legislation requires of women who have unwillingly conceived is quite different from what child-support legislation requires of men who have unwillingly conceived. To be sure, such men must pay child support, but they are never forced to what lawyers call "specific performance." They aren't required by law to engage in the hands-on tasks of parenting: to change diapers, give baths, prepare and serve meals, help with homework, or take their children to soccer practice. Specific performance, in fact, is seen as a form of servitude that may lawfully be required of civilians (in the form of conscription) only when there is a danger to the state. It may not be imposed even on convicted felons. If a drunk driver smashes into your house, he might have to go to prison or pay for damages, but he doesn't have to repair your brickwork or replace your broken door with his own hands. If your employee breaks her contract with you by failing to rivet together the agreed-upon quota of widgets, you may fire her, but you can't chain her to the assembly line and force her to do the promised work.

Yet policy makers who want to outlaw abortion in effect draw a line between unwilling fathers and unwilling mothers. They want to hold pregnant women—who are innocent of any wrongdoing—to a punitive standard of specific performance. The women aren't forced, to be sure, to change diapers or give baths, but they're sentenced to the many kinds of purposeful activities that a human pregnancy entails. No other class of people is held to this standard in peacetime. No woman should be held to it either.

But, it's objected, this sort of argument pits a woman's right to bodily integrity against another's *life*. Surely life is more important than bodily integrity? If that's so, we might, I suppose, aim at gender equity by enacting a law that forces all able-bodied men to donate a kidney to someone who will die without one. That way, they, too, would have to do something with their bodies to support someone else's life—something a little like the creative, agential work that women do when they sustain a pregnancy. When that law is passed, it might be fair to hold women to the specific performance of forced pregnancy. Until then, it's hard to see proposals to ban abortion as anything other than a gender-biased form of state-imposed slavery.

In a riff on Judith Jarvis Thomson's famous argument distinguishing between everyone's right to life and no one's right to the use of another person's body to sustain life (1971), Little contends that the fetus's right to life, if it exists, is as circumscribed as any other right. According to John Stuart Mill's Liberty Principle, famously, our freedom to act extends no further than the point where it causes another's harm. My right to swing my fist, as they say, stops at your chin. And if that's so for undisputed rights bearers, it would presumably also be true for fetuses: their rights would end where the woman's right to bodily integrity begins (Little 1999, 298).

Many people have sympathy for these liberty concerns in cases where sex was forced on the woman, but cases where the woman engages in sex voluntarily can prompt a different intuition—that consent to intercourse is consent to pregnancy. Everybody knows that sex is a risky business, so, as your mother probably told you, if you don't want to have his baby, stay out of the backseat of his car. But there's no good reason to think that inviting this man to penetrate me means I've invited this fetus to occupy me. For one thing, my hospitality was extended to the man, not the fetus, and apart from special circumstances, hospitality isn't transitive (which is why you may not attend the White House dinner just because your uncle, who hates the president's politics, passed his own invitation on to you). For another, there is a difference between consenting to a somewhat risky undertaking and deciding what to do if the risk should materialize. "To assume the risk of impregnation is not the same as consenting to gestate rather than abort if I do become pregnant," notes Little, "any more than assuming the risk of lung cancer by smoking means that I consent to surgery rather than palliative care should I get the disease" (Little 1999, 303). All these considerations—of consent, bodily integrity, what a right to life actually encompasses, and specific performance—explain why the legal right to abortion must be protected.

The Moral Permissibility of Abortion

Recognizing a legal right to abortion is one thing. It's quite another, though, to sort out when it's morally permissible to *exercise* that right. Many reservations about abortion, after all, are grounded in the idea that mothers have special responsibilities to their children, with the attendant thought that if the fetus has a claim on anything, surely it has a claim on its mother to preserve and protect it. But this way of thinking supposes that a maternal relationship has already been established. If it had, and if the relationship were one of paradigmatic parenthood (rather than, say, the one a birth mother has with a child she's given up for adoption, or a birth father has with a child he seldom sees), the argument that duties of love and hands-on care inhere in the relationship would make a certain amount of sense. However, as Little points out, there is a moral difference between the duties that attach to an already-existing relationship, and those, if any, a person might have to pursue such a relationship in the first place. She argues that at the start of a pregnancy—when, for example, a woman sits on the back stoop with her coffee in the dawn, fresh in the knowledge of the life growing inside her—the question on the table is whether she's morally obligated to *forge* that relationship, not what's required because she's in it.

Some people, Little observes, have a stronger claim on one's willingness to form a relationship with them than others: you may refuse an overture of friendship from the passenger in the seat next to you, but you must be open to some sort of connection with your in-laws. This is not to say you must *pursue* the connection with your in-laws; you might have a very good reason for not doing so (their notoriety as career criminals, for example). The point is merely that we owe more openness to some prospective relationships than to others. And the biological link to a fetus, Little thinks, creates just such a claim on our openness (Little 1999, 307).

It's a modest enough claim, no more than a bid that you consider carefully whether you have room in your life and heart for the child this fetus could become, and that seems plausible enough. Yet even in the small class of cases where a claim on your openness exists, you don't automatically have to honor it—especially when the relationship under contemplation is both prolonged and physically and emotionally enmeshed. You aren't, to take an analogous instance, required to accept a marriage proposal from even a long-standing suitor, although, at a minimum, you are ordinarily obliged to take his offer seriously. You certainly owe him your reasons for refusing, as the kind of connection already established between you likely gave rise to expectations that the suit would be favorably received. And while your fetus isn't the kind of thing to which you could owe reasons for refusing, the fact that it's yours, in your body, so that you are uniquely positioned to do the work of turning it into something of enormous value, does seem to require you to consider carefully before you turn away from the gestational relationship.

If this is right, it gives us a way to make sense of the abortion intuition—"I think abortions should be legal, but *I* could never have one." *You* have three other suitors you like equally well, and you aren't sure you could make a success of marriage in any case, so you should refuse. *I* am deeply in love and want to share my life with my beloved, so I couldn't possibly refuse. And of course, a difference between the intimacies of marriage and those of motherhood is that motherhood need not be monogamous, and so (naively but intelligibly): I could never refuse.

What troubles me about Little's account is that she seems to suggest that even if certain kinds of connections require openness to certain kinds of intimacy, the claim to an intimate relationship can always be refused. She writes,

> Personal relationships are partly constituted by emotions and interconnection of psyche. The claim someone presents thus cannot be a direct claim that I enter the relationship, fully formed, but a claim that I be open to those connections—to

interactions, say, that could lead to their development. None of this is to say I must pursue the relationship or the interactions; there are all sorts of legitimate reasons for declining, including, crucially, how much space I have in my life. (Little 1999, 307)

The voluntaristic nature of these observations seems best suited for relations among equals—the independent social contractors, radically unencumbered by ties to other people, that most liberal political and moral theories were developed to deal with. Little is careful to begin her essay by pointing out how firmly this picture of persons has held philosophers captive and how inapt it is as a representation of a gestating woman. Yet here, in her discussion of intimacy, might she have been captured by it herself?

Not all of us are powerful, unattached agents, free to choose our intimate relations. Some of us—children, severely disabled adults, frail elderly people—are in positions of dependency, relying on others to create and maintain the structures of intimacy in which we can receive needed care. Others of us—any capable person, really—can find ourselves thrust into an intimate relationship because someone in a position of dependency makes a claim on us, their need is great, and there is no one else to help. A third kind of unchosen intimacy occurs among those who are thrown into close proximity for lengthy periods of time: siblings who are reared together, army buddies, prisoners, and the like. Some of these are relationships we all must enter at least for a while, whether we will or not, and they all give rise to moral claims of one sort or another. These claims might be outright duties, or more the kind of thing that, if I don't do them, I'm just not behaving very well, but they all exert some degree of moral pull. So if we are going to take the intimate nature of pregnancy seriously, we have to consider whether it more closely resembles unchosen relationships than elective ones.

Here we return to the difference between the architect and the bee. In nonhuman animals, for all we can tell, pregnancy is a process that occurs in the female without any purposive contributions on her part: she passively suffers the fetus to grow in her rather than actively shaping it, so the relationship that ensues is a purely biological one. In human pregnancies, by contrast, what begins as a purely biological relationship is transformed into a recognizably human one because, by what the woman does in word, deed, and imagination, she calls her fetus into personhood. It's not until *after* she starts doing this that the fetus becomes the sort of entity with whom personal relations are even possible. Only then is it the child, sister, or grandson to whom I might be tied, though I did not choose to be.

This is to repeat that the woman watching in the dawn cannot step into *any* kind of ready-made relationship with her fetus, whether chosen or unchosen, because the relationship doesn't exist until she creates it. What she is doing on the stoop, rather, is accepting the invitation to begin building it.

Not everyone, of course, finds considerations of this kind persuasive; many women think of the fetus as nothing more than a lump of tissue that can be removed for any old reason or no reason at all. Others are convinced that all abortions are morally wrong. When such women find themselves unwillingly pregnant due to rape, accident, lack of access to contraception, or a conviction that contraception, too, is immoral, yet can't bring themselves to abort the fetus, they have no alternative but to continue the pregnancy. Which is to say, they must create a relationship they didn't choose. For them, the picture of the unencumbered, socially powerful, free agent so beloved by liberal moral theorists is a particularly inapt fit, but even if the invitation to intimacy in their case is more in the nature of a royal command, some manage to reconcile themselves to the pregnancy or even come to see it, despite its nonvolitional nature, as a blessing all the same.

If, on the other hand, a woman can't overcome her unwilling-ness to be a mother, or she'd like to be a mother but she just doesn't have the resources to rear the child she believes she's required to gestate, then her best option is to give it up for adoption at birth. But the cost of doing this must be taken much more seriously than anti-abortion rhetoric typically represents it to be. Consider: for nine months, the woman has created a bond of intense intimacy with this entity that she daily brings closer to personhood. The intimacy needn't be loving, though she may find she can't help but love, but whether she loves it, hates it, or harbors no feeling at all toward it, her fetus is thoroughly entwined with her, tied as tightly to her as any other human being can possibly be tied. At birth, then, she will have to break that tie, which, for many, is to do violence not only to it but to herself.

CALLING INTO PERSONHOOD

But we anticipate. Let's return to the moment at the end of our story, when the young woman on the stoop has accepted the pregnancy. Did she do the morally right thing? Did the reasons for acting, in the language of moral particularism, cluster into a "good-making" shape? Her strongest reason seems to be the need to hold herself in her own identity: she couldn't turn away this invitation to build a new relationship and still be who she is. And if that's how the reason behaves here, in this moment, outweighing or silencing all the rea-sons in her life that point to an abortion and in this way serving as the organizational focus of the moral shape of the situation she finds herself in, then yes, she's doing what's right.

So now she is ready to start initiating her fetus into the practice of personhood. It's a purely one-sided activity—the fetus hasn't yet developed the personality to which it will give bodily expression when born, and in any case, she couldn't recognize that expression even if it existed, much less respond to it. So what she does instead is call to it, by making physical arrangements for it, creating social space for it, and thinking of it as if it were already the born child she hopes it will become.

William Ruddick has usefully called the forward-looking relationship established in this way a *proleptic* relationship. Prolepsis, as a literary device, is the treating of a future state of affairs as if it already existed. It's achieved by means of an anticipatory adjective, as in the poetic "While yon slow oxen turn the furrowed plain," where the plain won't actually be furrowed until later, after the oxen have finished turning it. Proleptic *pregnancies* also anticipate the future in this way, because the mother-to-be treats the fetus as if it had already attained personhood. It's not uncommon in the course of a pregnancy, for example, for the woman to give the fetus a nickname (my daughter's fetus was called Pigwidgeon in utero, though the baby turned out to look nothing at all like an owl), and all sorts of other activities, from furnishing a nursery to starting a college fund, are apt to take place in the months before the child is actually born. Ruddick dubs the proleptic view of pregnancy the "maternalist" conception, because the gestating woman thinks of the pregnancy as a maternal project of (active) baby making, not (passive) baby carrying (Ruddick 2000, 97). Note how, in accepting the pregnancy and beginning the process of calling to her fetus, the woman adds an important set of stories to her own self-conception.[2] She now not only bears the identity of a pregnant woman but also

2. I thank Byron J. Stoyles for reminding me to make this explicit.

becomes a particular *kind* of pregnant woman: she is a (fittingly proleptic) expectant mother.

It's not just the woman herself who engages her baby-to-be proleptically. Her family, friends, coworkers, health care providers, and strangers on the street all do it, too: "Is it a boy or a girl?" "How's it going, Mama?" "I've brought you some clothes for the baby." Nor is it just individuals who call to the fetus in this way. The entire society mobilizes to help the gestating woman turn her fetus into a person. The pregnancy triggers an elaborate set of formal and informal social mechanisms whose sole purpose is, in one way or another, to call the fetus into personhood.

To see how these mechanisms work, it's helpful to bear in mind that identities—perhaps especially the pregnant woman's identity—set up socially shared normative expectations. Recall that our identities serve as guides for what we are supposed to do, and we treat ourselves and others according to our narrative understanding of who we and they are. Many of the narratives that constitute the identities of pregnant women are personal and particular: they are the stories of the two miscarriages you suffered before this pregnancy was finally established, or how you were planning to fall out of the drunk tree at the New Year's Eve party and hit all the branches on the way down but decided you'd better do a pregnancy test just in case and omigod it was positive—or how you got up in the dawn to consider the possibility of an abortion. More of the stories, though, are the master narratives, ubiquitous in movies, TV, magazines, and other media, that show pregnant women undertaking what in the United States has become an astonishingly large number of material and mental practices: announcing the pregnancy to family and friends, watching what they eat and drink, posting status updates on Facebook, putting themselves under a doctor's care, buying or borrowing baby furniture and clothing, reading *What to Expect When You're Expecting*, talking about their pregnancies and plans for delivery to sometimes even the most casual acquaintances, putting wish lists on the Target and Babies "R" Us gift registries, monitoring their blood pressure regularly, and on and on and on. Although these narratives purport merely to *represent* pregnant women as engaging in the practices, in fact, many of them are highly normative, shot through with "oughts," "shoulds," and "mustn'ts." If you do not do the things they prescribe, you are lazy, neglectful, selfish, or dangerous—in short, you are a morally bad mother, open to others' censure and sometimes to legal sanctions.[3]

Most of the master narratives about pregnancy currently circulating in the United States depict the good pregnant woman as vigilantly guarding her bodily purity so as to provide an unsullied environment for her growing fetus. If she's a smoker, these stories tell her to quit; if she's an addict, they tell her to get into rehab. They tell her to refrain from ingesting alcoholic and other adult beverages. They tell her to stop taking antihistamines and other over-the-counter drugs and start taking vitamins. They tell her to get enough rest and exercise and to monitor her weight. They tell her to

> avoid an array of foods from soft cheese to sushi, to sleep in a specified position (currently, avoiding stomach and back, with left side preferred to right), to avoid paint (including those with low volatile compounds), to avoid changing the cat litter, not to sit in the bathtub longer than ten minutes, not to sample the cookie dough, to avoid loud music, and even to keep a laptop computer several inches from [her] pregnant bell[y], "just in case." (Lyerly et al. 2009, 38)

---

3. For just one of a great many examples, the *New York Times* reported the case of a woman in Florida (why is it always Florida?) whose doctor recommended bed rest because she was at risk for a miscarriage. When the woman protested that she had two toddlers to care for and a job, the doctor alerted the state and a circuit court judge ordered her to bed (*NYT*, January 21, 2010).

They tell her to get to know the master narratives themselves: to surf pregnancy blogs and enter pregnancy chat rooms, to talk to friends, buy books, watch TV, and read magazines to acquire further information about what she may or must not put into her body. Most of all, they tell her to submit herself to the professional health care system where experts can monitor her body to ensure a healthy pregnancy.

Master narratives are essential for human social life; without them, we wouldn't know what we are supposed to do. But because they work on us subliminally, at a visceral rather than a rational level, they tend to be evidence resistant: facts that call them into question are generally silenced and get little uptake. For example, there is simply no evidence that moderate consumption of alcohol while pregnant is harmful to the fetus (Armstrong 2004),[4] and Lyerly and colleagues' list of forbidden substances and activities likewise carries no evidence of harm; indeed, some of the items actually carry evidence of safety. Yet because pregnant women's behavior is policed by others acting on the basis of these narratives and the women themselves frequently internalize them, they are likely to find that *even if they know the countervailing evidence,* they can't bring themselves to put into their bodies anything they wouldn't feed their born children—"just in case."

The master narrative of the dangerously permeable maternal body has played an active role in pregnant women's identities for many thousands of years. Noting that over 80 percent of the subheadings under "pregnancy" in an academic library catalogue pertain to women's ingestion of substances deemed harmful to fetuses, Rebecca Kukla comments that contemporary culture seems no different from the premodern and modern era in placing the blame for

---

4. The master narrative of the good pregnant woman as teetotaler gets particularly vigorous uptake. I once saw a total stranger walk up to a visibly pregnant woman in a bar and take the glass of wine out of her hand, as the other denizens of the bar murmured their indignant approval.

deformed babies squarely on women's passions and cravings (Kukla 2005, 106). "Across history," she writes, "we have worried about what pregnant women eat, breathe, drink, and absorb, and (more or less vividly at different moments in history) even with what they see, smell, wish, and imagine, insofar as all these ingestions risk polluting the space of the womb" (Kukla 2005, 6).

Notice how *proleptic* the anxiety about purity is: the fetus is treated, not only by the woman but also by her health care providers and all the others who take it on themselves to monitor her behavior, as if it were already its own independent entity, living inside the woman but separate from her in a way it won't actually be until after she has given birth. In 1965, this tendency to prolepsis was given a visual boost when Lennart Nilsson's endoscopic fetal images appeared with much fanfare in what became a landmark issue of *Life* magazine. Since then, representations of fetuses out of the womb, looking like born babies, can be found in everything from antiabortion posters, to *2001: A Space Odyssey*, to car ads, to ultrasound pictures on the refrigerator door.

Barbara Katz Rothman (1993) and Barbara Duden (1993) are only two of the many scholars who have pointed out that these images are grossly misleading, not only because they erase the woman whose body they grow in but also because they are artfully edited to maximize the fetuses' resemblance to attractive human babies. These objections are valid ones: to the extent that the images downplay the active role the woman takes in gestation, they belittle her and thereby constrict her agency, while the contrived likeness to born children is easily and often co-opted into an argument for why fetuses must never be aborted. On the other hand, because fetuses that will become born children must be called into personhood not only by their mothers but also by the rest of society, it's easy enough to see how these proleptic images aid in that endeavor. Like many practices that are oppressive to women, this one is not without genuine social value. There's no good reason, though, why the wider society has to call fetuses into personhood in such a way as to diminish the contribution of those who do the lion's share of it.

IDENTITY AND PERSONHOOD

I've suggested that calling a fetus into personhood centrally involves forging an identity for the child the fetus will become and that this is typically the responsibility in particular of the gestating woman. To see why, it might help to recall that personhood, as I have been conceptualizing it, is a social practice consisting of four necessary moments:

1. A human being feels, watches, wonders, thinks, or in some other respect engages in the mental activity that gives rise to her personality.
2. The mental activity finds bodily expression.
3. Another human being recognizes it as the expression of a personality
4. And responds.

This is a social practice because it is rule governed and dependent on a great many other social practices and institutions for its existence. With the possible exception of people with certain forms of autism or severe cognitive disability, participation in the practice quickly becomes second nature: we do it without thinking, automatically or, as we say, naturally. The four moments are separable only analytically. In practice, they usually occur close to simultaneously among all the persons in a given encounter.

Identity enters into the practice at all four moments. (1) The many states of mind crossing my consciousness include characteristic ways of putting the world together, reacting to situations, thinking about things or taking them for granted, worrying or being optimistic, setting standards for myself, and so on, that contribute to the self that I am. Some of them are so characteristic of me that they enter into my self-conception: I use the plot templates and character types of master narratives, as well as other stories, to represent these states to myself as a way of making sense of who I am, and in doing so, I engage in one part of the first-person work of sustaining my identity. Notice that I draw the fragments of master narratives from the common store, so that even from my own first-person perspective, my identity is socially constructed: it depends crucially on the cultural resources available to me. My self-conception is itself a set of images and story fragments that cross my consciousness: my characteristic way of understanding who I am is a part of my personality that is, in turn, capable of depiction in story form.

My self-conception is not, of course, infallible. I can be somewhat or entirely mistaken in supposing that a given way of thinking or feeling is in fact characteristic of me; I could, for example, be a sore loser who sees myself as a good sport.

(2) Giving these states of mind physical expression makes them public. Many such expressions are spontaneous: crying, shrugging, relaxing, laughing, following a person with one's eyes. Others have to be taught: speaking, writing, cooking, bearing oneself proudly, performing music, sitting like a lady. Some are open only to certain kinds of people; I can properly express my resentment at your disobedience, for example, only if I'm in a position to be obeyed. Much of what I express has nothing to do with my identity, but some of it does—it's the raw data out of which others form their sense of me. If I often express resentment, for example, others will correctly

characterize me as a resentful person, though my desire to think well of myself might keep me from seeing myself that way. Moreover, I act on the basis of the stories that form my self-conception, and in doing so, I also express who I think I am.

I can, of course, be somewhat or very clumsy in how I express myself. I can also deliberately mislead others into thinking I'm somebody I'm not.

(3) Once my mental activity receives expression, it becomes possible for others to read it off my body and thus to register that I have a personality, that I am a person. This kind of reading almost always takes training; we'll see in the next chapter the few instances that are innate. For example, even babies recognize a smile, but children have to be educated to see a smile as welcoming, amused, or scornful. Later, they learn when "Oh, it's no trouble at all" means exactly the opposite; later still, they may come to understand what a particular choice of clothing, in a particular context, says about a person. When we recognize the expression of a human personality, what we recognize is never just a person, but a person of a certain *kind*. I use the master narratives that contribute to the identities of people of that kind to make whatever sense I must of this person here before me: "little girl," "police officer," "cyclist." When it's a stranger I pass on the street, these crude sortings usually suffice, as I have no need to fine-tune the person's identity further. When I must interact with people on a regular basis, though, I need to get a better sense of who they are—recall that identities set up the normative expectations that let me know how I may or must treat them. Whether personal stories will join the master narratives that make up my understanding of the person depends on the kind of relationship I have with her. If she's my wife, I'll have a thick, deep sense of who she is, made up of many stories of both kinds. If he's been my coworker for a couple of years, I probably won't know him

as well, but at a minimum, a few personal stories of my interactions with him will accompany the master narratives that constitute his identity from my third-person perspective. How I identify another sometimes depends on how I identify myself, and in that way, too, identity enters into the third moment. Dovey Whitehead, for example, can be simultaneously Miz Potts's daughter, my student, Bubba's wife, and Lucy Mae's mother, but if I see myself as part of an "us" that is far superior to Dovey's "them," I might dismiss Dovey as trailer trash. Recognitions of this kind are epistemically, socially, and morally normative, but the norms don't always comfortably coincide. In identifying Dovey as I do, I may be adhering to a social norm in my part of the world at the same time as I have clearly violated a moral one.

I can, then, be somewhat or entirely mistaken in how I represent a person. I can also, as we'll see later, deliberately refuse to see him as he truly is.

(4) Identities offer normative guidance: my sense of who others are, juxtaposed with my sense of who I am, tells me how I am supposed to respond to them (and, of course, how they are supposed to respond to me). Some social practices are designed to help me identify the person properly: she wears a maid's uniform so that when she opens the door to me, I don't treat her as my host's daughter; he occupies the inner office so that I won't mistake him for the receptionist. Even without these cues, I know to respond to her as a person-in-general—in that I don't sit or step on her, for example, or carve her up for my Sunday dinner—but to the extent that I interact with her at all, I do so out of the narrative constructions that allow me to make sense of what *kind* of person she is, and these are my third-person contribution to her identity. As the example of Dovey indicates, I also treat her out of the narrative constructions that constitute my contribution to my own identity.

Christine Korsgaard has usefully developed the notion of a "practical identity":

> a description under which you value yourself, a description under which you find your life to be worth living and your actions to be worth undertaking.... Practical identity is a complex matter and for the average person there will be a jumble of such conceptions. You are a human being, a woman or a man, an adherent of a certain religion, a member of an ethnic group, a member of a certain profession, someone's lover or friend, and so on. And all of these identities give rise to reasons and obligations. (Korsgaard 1996, 101)

Many—possibly even most—practical identities are reciprocal (teacher and student, doctor and patient, father and daughter, clerk and customer), and the norms attending them govern the resulting relationship. My being Dovey's teacher gives me reasons to assign her readings, explain the course material to her, comment on her papers in a timely fashion, and so on.

I can, of course, fail to do these things or not do them well, in which case I am a bad teacher.

THE PRIMARY IDENTITY GIVER

If personhood is the ground on which personal identity rests, and if I'm right about what the practice of personhood consists of, then it's pretty clear that fetuses can't be persons—they are too well hidden for any of us except possibly the women carrying them to make out anything of their personalities or to identify them in any very specific ways. Even in the third trimester, only the first of the four moments of the practice of personhood has got a foothold, so none of the identity-work that enters into the practice can be carried out.

By then, however, the pregnant woman typically gains an increasing sense of her fetus as a distinct entity that she is *carrying* inside her body, rather than being somehow merged with it. And the routine use of ultrasound for fetal monitoring has made it increasingly likely that she will know the fetus's sex. So in the ordinary way of things, although perhaps not if she is giving the child up for adoption, the closer she comes to the end of the pregnancy, the more apt she is to weave around her fetus the narrative fragments that serve as its protoidentity. Mostly, these will be stories of relationship—narratives that identify the child to come as my (our) son or daughter, a Potts, a direct descendant of Thomas Jefferson, a Southerner. But the tissue of stories also contains master narratives by which she makes sense of the fact that the child will belong to a minority race in a racist society, or be a girl, or be deaf, and so on. And the personal stories of how she came to be pregnant, what her lover did when she told him, her reflections on the stoop—all these enter into the protoidentity as well. At this point in the pregnancy, when the fetus is still inside the woman's body but now actively moving about, the woman is constantly aware of it as no one around her can be. That awareness, coupled with the unrelieved intimacy of her relationship with it, encumbers her with the lion's share of the work of forging the coming child's identity.

In this chapter, I've used the abortion intuition to motivate the idea that human pregnancy is a purposeful, creative activity that sets into motion a great many normative social practices, among them, the proleptic practices and acts of imagination by which fetuses are called into personhood. I've tried to show how identities are integral to personhood and why fetal identities are too rudimentary to get a purchase on it. Now it's time to examine how children are initiated into personhood and how their identities are forged. We'll also look at how children learn to hold others in their identities and what kinds of holding are open to them from a very young age.

Chapter 3

Second Persons

The Work of Identity Formation

Persons essentially are *second* persons who grow up with other persons.

—Annette Baier

The little boy in the bright red sweater took his sister's hand, trotting to keep up with her as she made for the trees at the edge of the park, away from the picnic table where the grownups were so busy talking they paid no attention to what the children were doing. Dandelions were sprinkled across the brilliant green grass like cheerful yellow pennies, while the pale spring sun overhead provided just enough warmth to counteract the fresh breeze ruffling the children's hair— hers so fair it was almost white, his darker and sticking up no matter how much his mother brushed it down. A squirrel, dashing by on business of its own, stopped to look at them. The boy wanted to return the look but his sister single-mindedly pulled him on.

When they reached the edge of the park, however, she slowed down. Here the grass gave way to oak, beech, and maple trees, their young yellow-green leaves making lace against the blue sky. Ahead, the undergrowth on either side of the asphalt path was not yet as dense as it would be later in the year, and, deeper in the woods, a few patches of white and pink marked plum and redbud trees in bloom. Little clearings and rabbit roads wound among the trees, forming inviting tunnels through the foliage and leading nowhere in particular.

"See all the trails, Jack-Jack? We can be explorers, and go exploring. I'll be the leader. We're gonna go find the creek. You don't have to worry about getting lost 'cause I can easily find the way back."

"Daddy said to stay in the playground," Jack answered doubtfully.

"I know," his sister explained patiently. "But he wouldn't have said that if he knew how easily I can find the way back. You couldn't do it by yourself because you're too little, but when you're with me you can do it 'cause I'll take care of you, okay?"

"Okay, Ellie."

The children accordingly left the path and made their way through the undergrowth, ducking under the branches, stepping around the clusters of violets, squelching through the puddles, and stopping to watch with interest as a toad hopped out from under a fern. They tried to catch it, but it disappeared into the woods, so they gave it up and found another trail, one that led them on in an entirely new direction. Soon, however, the ground began to slope gently downhill, and presently they came to a clump of rhododendrons that completely blocked their path. When they had worked their way through this, they found themselves at the edge of a steep bank, at the bottom of which was a shallow creek, flecked with sunshine, that bubbled and gurgled along a rocky bed.

"We found it! We found it!" Ellie shouted. "C'mon, Jack-Jack!" Not stopping to wait for him, she got down on her hands and knees and, grabbing at roots and branches to steady herself, scrambled down the muddy slope. After considerable coaxing, and driven only by the fear of being left behind, the little boy followed. It's true that he lost his footing halfway down and slid the rest of the way on his stomach, but Ellie set him on his feet with such loud praise that he decided not to cry and started laughing instead.

Ellie laughed, too, and showed him how to throw pebbles into the water. Then he threw a stick and was enchanted to see it floating along the surface instead of sinking. They followed the stick downstream until it lodged itself gently against a tangle of roots, which it did almost at once. The children then lost interest, but just below that spot, where a fallen branch had attracted a clump of vegetation that impeded the flow of the water, they found a miniature pool or backwater, home to a family of minnows. "Fish!" Ellie cried, and squatted to catch one. "Fish!" echoed Jack, and squatted to catch one, too. They were still at this fascinating occupation some ten minutes later, when they heard voices calling.

"It's Daddy," Ellie told Jack, and then, "Coming, Daddy!" She grabbed the little boy's hand and pulled him, protesting, away from the water. But the bank, high enough upstream at the point where they descended, was here so steep that they could find no way up. They retraced their steps until they found a more navigable route where, Ellie boosting Jack and he scrambling wildly, they made their way back to the top.

Nothing looked familiar. Ahead was a glade, thickly carpeted with ferns; on either side were more trees and bushes. The only sounds they heard were birdcalls and the gurgling of the creek. "We'll go this way," Ellie decided on no grounds at all, and they plunged into the woods.

After what seemed like a long time, she saw a break through the trees. "I think the park should be right through there." Jack, who had been looking increasingly anxious, broke into a grin and ran ahead, but when he reached the spot, it was only another clearing—larger than the others they had passed, it's true, but certainly not the park.

"Are we lost?" he asked.

"Well, it's s'posed to *be* here!" said Ellie. "But don't be afraid, Jack-Jack. I'll take care of you."

"What do we do?"

"Let's shout. Maybe Daddy will hear us."

They shouted, and kept shouting until they were tired, but nothing happened. Finally, Ellie's lower lip started to tremble, which frightened Jack, and before they knew it, both children began to cry. This, though useless from a purely practical point of view, relieved their feelings. Presently, Ellie pulled herself together and looked around her. Off in the distance, visible between the trees, was something that looked like a fence. "There's something over there," she said, pointing. "Maybe it's somebody's yard and there's somebody there and they can help us."

"I'm going to shout some more," said Jack. "Daddy! Maaaaaa-ma!" But he followed her through the underbrush. What they found when they got there was not a fence, but something much better: the weather-beaten wooden rail that ran along the asphalt path leading out of the woods. In one direction, they could see the stream, so they went the other way, and, in what seemed an eternity but was actually only half an hour, they emerged into the park.

There were Mama and Aunt Lori with Baby Sylvia, surrounded by park rangers, and then Mama was running and when she got to them she was sobbing and laughing and hugging them so hard they couldn't breathe. She let go of them to pull her phone out of her pocket. "They're here! Yeah, they just walked out of the woods. Yes, honey, really—they're all right. Okay, I'll wait."

The immediate need was for a toilet, and when that was taken care of, Mama produced drinks and cookies left over from the picnic. The rangers had some, too, and then they went away, and Daddy and Uncle Eric emerged from the trees. Daddy hugged them almost as hard as Mama had done, and when he set them down, he put his arm around Mama and said, "You know we were looking for you for over an hour, don't you?"

Ellie twisted herself into a pretzel, and Jack inspected his fingers. Neither child said anything. Daddy crouched down to their eye level, studied their muddy, tear-stained faces and their muddy, wet shoes, and shook his head. "Mama and I aren't going to yell at you. But you scared us. A lot. Can you tell us what happened?"

The children squirmed.

"Okay," said Mama, "Let's start with your clothes. You first, Jack-Jack. How did you get mud all down your sweater?"

Jack gave her a quick little grin. "We saw fishes."

"Fish?" Mama looked at Ellie.

"Yes, Mama. There were tiny little baby fish in a little pool. They were swimming."

"And what's that got to do with Jack's sweater?"

"Well, he fell down. But he didn't get hurt, did you, Jack?"

Jack shook his head. "We saw fishes, Daddy."

"And there was a frog," said Ellie. "Remember the frog, Jack-Jack? It was under some leaves and it hopped right out at us but we didn't catch it because it was too hoppy."

"A frog," Jack echoed.

Daddy sat down on the picnic bench. "We had no idea where you went. You knew that, right?"

"Well, yes, Daddy, but I could easily find the way back. You wouldn't have said to stay in the playground if you knew I could easily find the way back, but I knew I could, though."

Daddy's glance stopped her. "Was it easy?"

Ellie didn't answer.

Daddy's blue eyes remained steadily fixed on her. "Ellie, you and Jack got lost."

Ellie blinked very fast and bit the insides of her cheeks, but it was no good. Her face crumpled, her fists flew to her eyes, and she cried as if her heart would break. Jack, sorely troubled, put his arms around her. "I was so scared," she hiccupped, as soon as she was able to draw breath. "I didn't know where we were and I had to take care of Jack-Jack and you didn't ever come and I thought it would be nighttime soon and then a big scary monster would get us and we'd d-d-die."

Mama knelt and pulled them both close. "Oh, honey. Oh, my poor sweet babies. We'll always come, always. Sometimes it just takes us a while." She was close to tears herself. "We should have kept a better eye on you."

"Well, anyway, you did find your way back in the end," said Daddy. "So that was pretty smart. How'd you do it?"

But as the children didn't really know, they couldn't say.

So they helped to carry the picnic things back to the car, said goodbye to Baby Sylvia, allowed Aunt Lori and Uncle Eric to give them each a hug, and climbed into the backseat of the car. Jack fell asleep on the way home, but Ellie was quiet, immensely comforted by the sound of the grown-ups talking up in front.

SECOND NATURE

As the children's misadventure in the woods reminds us, there is something unnatural about the practices of responsibility that make up our moral lives, so that knowing what we ought to do is no guarantee that we'll do it. Even three-year-old Jack knows that he and Ellie should have stayed on the playground, despite their desire to go exploring, while Daddy and Mama certainly knew they should have kept a closer watch over their children, despite their desire to enjoy themselves with the other adults. What is particularly striking about human beings, however, is not that they sometimes give in to their natural inclinations, but the many ways they successfully *resist* them. We mostly tell the truth even when it would be more convenient not to; we mostly refrain from stealing things we covet even when we could get away with it. In fact—and astonishingly enough—we do all sorts of things that go against the grain without having to give them even a moment's thought. They become, as we say, second nature.

But what is second nature? We owe the concept to Aristotle, so I'll start my account of it there. In his *Nicomachean Ethics*, he tells us that virtue of character requires a properly formed intellect. Morality, on his view, involves reasons for action, and these exist independently of our awareness of them, whether or not we are responsive to them. We come to see what those reasons are by acquiring "practical wisdom" (*phronesis*)—the faculty that lets us recognize and reflect on the rational requirements of morality and opens our eyes to the system of concepts and ways of proceeding that make the demands of morality intelligible to us. *Phronesis,* Aristotle says, is "a true disposition accompanied by rational prescription, relating to action in the sphere of what is good and bad for human beings" (1140b, 5–6).

We acquire *phronesis* by a decent upbringing, which instills in us good habits. "We must start," says Aristotle, "from what is knowable to us. Consequently, in order to listen appropriately to discussion about what is fine and just...one must have been well brought up. For the starting point is *that* it is so, and if this were sufficiently clear to us—well, in that case there will be no need to know in addition *why*. But such a person either has the relevant first principles, or might easily grasp them" (1095b, 4–9). This upbringing is crucial, for we are not naturally virtuous: "None of the excellences of character comes about in us by nature; for no natural way of being is changed through habituation.... The excellences develop in us neither by nature nor contrary to nature, but because we are naturally able to receive them and are brought to completion by means of habituation" (1103a, 20–26).

Notice that for Aristotle, ethical formation takes place within the *polis*. The well-ordered society provides the conditions under which sound moral training can take place: "But it is hard for someone to get the correct guidance towards excellence, from childhood on, if he has not been brought up under laws that aim at that effect; for a moderate and resistant way of life is not pleasant for most people, especially when they are young. So their upbringing and patterns of behaviour must be ordered by the laws; for these ways will not be painful to them if they have become used to them" (1179b, 31–36). Each of us, then, is dependent on the state, as well as some number of others, for the coaching, correcting, showing by example, and other forms of training by which we learn how to "do" morality. The habits of thought and action resulting from this training can be understood as second nature.

Rousseau, too, was interested in ethical formation, but he had a different problem: whereas Aristotle's difficulty was to explain how we can attain moral virtue if none of it arises in us by nature, Rousseau had to reconcile the Enlightenment insistence on self-legislation as the source of moral legitimacy with the need for social order. Dissatisfied with theories that looked to either God or nature as the ultimate ground of normativity, Enlightenment theorists sought to put morality on a secular and humanist footing. In Max Weber's fine term, Enlightenment nature became "disenchanted," emptied of the norms and values that on an Aristotelian ethics could anchor and justify moral claims. The free, autonomous individual answered to no one and nothing but himself, for only in that way could he be free.

But now the authority of the nation-state over its citizens became deeply problematic. If the individual made his own laws, it was hard to see how he could subject himself to the laws of another—whether imposed by majority vote, a constitutional legislator, or a tyrant. State legislation, it seemed, could only be contingent, legitimately binding individuals only if they happened to choose the same laws for themselves. As Rousseau famously put it, "The problem is to find a form of association which will defend and protect with the whole common force the person and goods of each associate, and in which each, while uniting himself with all, may still obey himself alone, and remain as free as before" (Rousseau 2003, 8-9).

The solution favored by most Enlightenment philosophers was to find a way for individuals to participate jointly in a "general will" that is both the will of each and the will of all, so that there could be no conflict between self-legislation and the laws of the state. Kant, for example, theorized that transcendental Reason dictates universally binding moral norms to which, on pain of irrationality, we must freely subject ourselves. For Hegel, the dialectically structured general will is *Geist* or Spirit, instantiated in human beings as "the habit of the ethical" and explicitly identified with second nature (Hegel 1991, 195). Rousseau's approach is something like Hegel's but not so transcendental: his picture of human beings was of earthbound, embodied, and passionate as well as rational individuals who are products of their time and place, so he couldn't look to universal Reason or Spirit to unite them. Instead, he argued that human beings' biological first natures must be remade, overlaid with socially inculcated *second* natures that incline them to choose principles of social cooperation. Because these choices are voluntary, they are free, and because they conduce to social harmony, they don't conflict with the laws of the state.

Like Aristotle, Rousseau assigns state legislators a large part of the responsibility for making second natures. In practice, though, as Rebecca Kukla persuasively argues, Rousseau assigns the lion's share of the work of shaping second nature to mothers. As soon as a child is born, its mother can start to transform it into a good citizen by how she feeds, dresses, speaks to, and disciplines it. Indeed, even in nursing her baby, the mother becomes the origin of the well-formed individual, physically transmitting her patriotism, through her milk, directly to the child (Kukla 2005, 31). As Rousseau's portrait of *Emile*'s Sophie makes abundantly clear, he considered women to be fairly dim-witted, but they are nevertheless fitted for shaping second nature because, on his sentimentalist and materialist view of human beings, second nature embraces far more than our rational nature. Instilling it is not just a matter of molding intellectual beliefs and commitments, but of working at a more fundamental, visceral level to shape "the sentiments, habits, passions, and bodily constitution... that lay the ground for our exercises of will, reason, and social participation" (Kukla 2005, 41).

McDowell's problem is more basic than either Aristotle's or Rousseau's. His question is not "How can we be moral?" or even "How can we have both freedom and social harmony?" but "How can rational beings exist in the natural world at all?" If, as the Enlightenment philosophers thought, nature is disenchanted, deprived of the meaningful relations that constitute rationality—if, that is to say, the "space of reasons," as McDowell calls it, has no connection whatever to the natural "realm of law"—then our minds can't be constrained by the world, and we have no way of justifying any of our beliefs about it. The natural realm could certainly cause us to have sensory experiences—I stub my toe on a rock, for example—but the content of our experience would be brutely natural, quite separate from the conceptual content proper to beliefs and judgments.

The "space of reasons" to which beliefs belong is constituted by "relations such as implication or probabilification" (McDowell 1996, 7). Beliefs are "spontaneous," in that we are free to rationally examine and change all the elements in our conception of the world, but they can be justified only by other beliefs. As Donald Davidson has it, "Nothing can count as a reason for holding a belief except another belief" (Davidson 1986, 310). And therein lies the difficulty. If the world is completely separate from the mind, it can't give us reasons for what we believe. And if the mind is completely separate from the world, then our beliefs are unbounded, free to fly off in every direction. They "degenerate into moves in a self-contained game" (McDowell 1996, 5) or "a frictionless spinning in a void" (McDowell 1996, 11). But surely judgments of nature as we experience it must be grounded in a way that relates them to a reality outside our minds, or they can't be a source of knowledge.

Worse still, given this opposition between the space of reasons and the realm of law, it becomes impossible to see how our sensory intake of the world, which we surely share with other natural animals, can be connected to conceptual thought. So what we have here are two problems: the problem of how conceptual thought can be *about* sensible nature and the problem of how minds can *exist* in sensible nature. Rationality threatens, as it were, to be "extruded" from nature, with no way to bridge the gap between the two.

McDowell's solution is to reflect on Aristotle's ethics. Rather than dualistically set the space of reasons over against our animal nature, he argues, we ought to appreciate the Aristotelian insight into our *second* nature as rational animals. When we do that, we can see that initiation into the space of reasons is simply an ordinary part of becoming mature adults. Through many kinds of socialization, our natural or animal processes (such as sensory perception) become infused with conceptual meaning: we distinguish the patch of lighter and darker blues from its surroundings and see it as a shirt. This "seeing as" produces knowledge because the world actually is organized according to the concepts by which we understand it: "For a perceiver with capacities of [reason]," he writes, "the environment is...the bit of objective reality that is within her perceptual and practical reach. It is that for her because she can conceive it in ways that display it as that" (116). On McDowell's view, then, the meaningless realm of law conceived as the object of modern natural science isn't all there is to nature. Nature also includes rational animals, whose second nature, acquired through initiation into the space of reason, gives them (us) a "foothold in the realm of law" and thereby sets welcome limits on the free interplay of ideas.

What all this amounts to is three distinct kinds of naturalization. Aristotle naturalizes morality: we are trained in early life to resist the inclinations of our first nature and acquire virtuous habits. Rousseau naturalizes social life: through early training and nurture, we come to participate in the general will. And McDowell naturalizes our rational relationship to the world: through initiation into the space of reasons, we come to take our place in, and transcend, the natural order. In these three ways, these philosophers naturalize what is so extraordinary about being human.

The Role of Language

How is it that we, born mere animals, are transformed into moral, political, rational agents who can go against our animal natures? Like McDowell, I believe that an absolutely central element in the socialization of human beings is the acquisition of language. It's in speaking to children: singing, commanding, exclaiming, making jokes, employing sarcasm, "requesting, thanking, cursing, greeting, praying" (Wittgenstein 2001, §23) that we not only open the gates for them to the space of reasons but also show them what to do when they get inside.

According to a number of developmental psychologists, including Vasudevi Reddy (2008), Peter Hobson (2003), and Michael Tomasello (2001), it's infants' connections with their caregivers that provide the basis for thought and language—especially creative symbolic thought. Such thinking requires us to take up multiple perspectives on something, which in turn requires learning to adopt at least one other person's perspective on it. And learning that perspective is possible only if we can identify emotionally with that person.

It begins with imitation. Babies as young as a month old imitate gestures, such as sticking out your tongue, but they also imitate emotions: when Aunt Lori smiles and looks happy, Baby Sylvia smiles. She knows that her mama's disgust feels like her disgust, and her mama's pain mirrors her own. One-year-olds go beyond emotions to imitate other people's desires: if they see you unsuccessfully try to pull a tube apart, they try to do it, too (Gopnik 2009, 205). And they imitate phonemes—the units of meaning-bearing sound that make up the words they hear. Between one and two, they start imitating the words that are spoken to them, and—importantly— at the same time they learn the conditions under which it's appropriate to say the words. So, for example, as Jack learns the words "thank you," he also learns he is supposed to say them when he is given something. (Learners' mistakes are possible, of course. I once knew a toddler who said "thank you" to whatever person or thing she took something from, including a bookshelf or the coffee table.)

Similarly, in learning the sorts of things that in picture books or real life go by the name of "cat," Jack learns far more than what a specific word means—he learns about his world.

There seems to be something about the continued acquisition of language that teaches children about other minds. By two or three, they explicitly attribute minds and mental activity to other people; they are happy when someone else gets what he wants, even if they don't want it themselves, and they're sad when he doesn't. But they don't yet understand *differences* between other people's minds and their own. A typical three-year-old who opens a candy box expects it to contain candy, so when it turns out to be full of pencils instead, he will be very surprised. Because he now knows what it contains, though, if you ask him what his absent friend will think is in the box, he'll confidently predict that she will know it's pencils, too. By the time they're five, children usually understand that others could have false beliefs— they say their absent friend will think the box contains candy. But deaf children born of hearing parents who don't use sign language are not likely to solve the problem of the candy box until they are eight or nine (Peterson and Siegal 1995).

Stanley Cavell explains what we learn along with language acquisition this way:

When you say "I love my love" the child may learn the meaning of the word 'love' and what love is. I.e., that (*what you do*) will *be* love in the child's world, and if it is mixed with resentment and intimidation, then love is a mixture of resentment and intimidation, and when love is sought *that* will be sought. When you say "I'll take you tomorrow, I promise," the child begins to learn what temporal durations are, and what trust is, and what you do will show what trust is worth. When you say "Put on your sweater," the child learns what commands are and what *authority* is, and if giving orders is something that creates anxiety for you, then authorities are anxious, authority itself uncertain. Of course, hopefully, the person, growing, will learn other things about these concepts and 'objects' also. They will grow gradually as the child's world grows. (Cavell 1961, 214)

Following Rules

If children begin to acquire language by imitation, they continue the process by mastering the rules for speaking a language. These rules govern the application of words, phrases, and sentences to appropriate contexts: Jack needs to learn not only the right way to say "thank you" but also the rules for saying it on the right occasions and to the right sort of entity. But how does he know when what he is doing accords with the rule he's been taught? Does the rule come with its own built-in rulebook that tells him whether he's followed it correctly? Does the rule somehow transcend all its particular applications, so that in grasping it, he always knows how to apply it?

Wittgenstein tells a peculiar little story to start us thinking about this. He asks us to imagine teaching a pupil how to write down some series of cardinal numbers of the form 0, n, 2n, 3n, etc., so that when we give him the order "+1," he writes 0, 1, 2, 3, etc.

Let us suppose we have done exercises and given him tests up to 1000.

Now we get the pupil to continue a series (say +2) beyond 1000—and he writes 1000, 1004, 1008, 1012.

We say to him: "Look what you've done!"—He doesn't understand. We say: "You were meant to add *two*: look how you've begun the series!"—He answers: "Yes, isn't it right? I thought that was how I was *meant* to do it.".. .

Such a case would present similarities with one in which a person naturally reacted to the gesture of pointing with the hand by looking in the direction of the line from finger-tip to wrist, not from wrist to finger-tip. (Wittgenstein 2001, §185)

Wittgenstein's point is that there's no reason, in principle, why 1,000 couldn't represent a threshold after which, to follow the +2 rule, you have to add twice-two—it's just that we don't do it that way. The line of thought culminates in "This was our paradox: no course of action could be determined by a rule, because every course of action can be made out to accord with the rule. The answer was: if everything can be made out to accord with the rule, then it can also be made out to conflict with it. And so there would be neither accord nor conflict" (§201).

In his usual fashion, Wittgenstein doesn't so much explain the paradox as put pressure on the Platonic and mentalistic pictures that underlie the demand for an explanation. By freeing ourselves of those pictures, we eliminate the need to look for external or internal standards of correctness beyond the actual application of the rule. You simply have to get a sense for how to go on when you reach 1,000 that accords with how everyone else does it, just as you have to understand that when I point with my finger, I want you to look away from my wrist, not toward it. (I have seen two-year-olds be confused about this.)

Wittgenstein speaks, not of language, but of "language-games," as a way of emphasizing "that the *speaking* of language is part of an activity, or form of life" (Wittgenstein 2001, §23). Initiation into a language is thus also initiation into the way we do things—our common behavior and shared modes of understanding.

Cavell puts Wittgenstein's point like this:

> We learn and teach words in certain contexts, and then we are
> expected, and expect others, to be able to project them into
> further contexts. Nothing insures that this projection will take
> place (in particular, not the grasping of universals nor the grasp-
> ing of a book of rules), just as nothing insures that we will make,
> and understand, the same projections. That on the whole we do
> is a matter of our sharing routes of interest and feeling, modes
> of response, senses of humor and of significance and of fulfill-
> ment, of what is outrageous, of what is similar to what else, what
> a rebuke, what forgiveness, of when an utterance is an assertion,
> when an appeal, when an explanation—all the whirl of organ-
> ism Wittgenstein calls "forms of life." Human speech and activity,
> sanity and community, rest on nothing more, but nothing less,
> than this. (Cavell 1969, 52)

When we begin to play a language game, we come to know the form
of life in which routes of interest and feeling, modes of response,
senses of humor and of significance and of fulfillment are shared. To
be sure, we learn the rational connections among concepts, but we
also acquire the things that undergird rationality: we get a sense for
what is ordinary or uncommon, what we can take for granted and
what requires investigation, how "we" carry on and how to tell who
counts as "we." It's in the initiation through language into a form of
life that we acquire our second natures.

Our second natures, then, give us our very selves: they make it
possible for us to live morally and sociably inside the space of reasons. Moreover, and just as fundamentally, our second natures give
us the world. They make our experiences of it intelligible, and this in

turn allows us to act purposefully in it, according to the reasons that are there.

SOCIAL KINDS

I have said that our ability to overcome the impulses and attitudes arising from our animal natures is, when you think about it, astonishing. So, too, is our ability to "do" identities—to express our individuality and at the same time to reveal our commonalities with others in the various social kinds to which we belong, to recognize others as unique individuals who also belong to social kinds, and to act on our own self-conceptions and to treat others according to our sense of who they are. This socially inflected identity-work also takes place in the space of reasons, and it, too, is part of our second natures.

Families are the primary sites of identity formation—a process that, as we saw in the last chapter, often begins before birth, as the family and other intimates proleptically call the fetus into personhood. As the child grows out of infancy, she *becomes* who she is through the mutual process of accommodating herself to her family and being accommodated by it (Minuchin 1974, 47–48), but she *understands* who she is—acquires the self-conception out of which she acts—by means of the stories that her parents and other family members use to constitute her identity and that they tacitly or explicitly teach her to apply to herself.

Among their many other functions, identities sort us into social kinds: male or female, straight or gay, middle-class or blue collar, able-bodied or disabled, black or white, and all the rest. But what are social kinds, exactly? If we're going to conceive of identities as narrative representations of selves, we need to understand what the stories that constitute them are actually depicting. What kind of property is the property of being middle-class? How natural or real is it? I'll argue that it's real enough—a social fact is, after all, a fact—but it's dependent on human thoughts, attitudes, and practices, and so it's a product of a particular time and place.

In a recent paper, Ásta Sveinsdóttir argues that the property of being a member of a social kind is a *conferred* property (Sveinsdóttir 2012). To see what she means by conferral, think of a strike in baseball. The ball travels a certain trajectory from the fingers of the pitcher to the glove of the catcher, but the physical property of traveling that trajectory isn't what makes it a strike. In fact, it isn't even the physical property plus the social conventions constituting the game of baseball that make it a strike. What makes a strike a strike is that the umpire says it is. Of course, the umpire's call is supposed to *track* the ball's flight, but even if the umpire was wrong about whether the ball was actually in the strike zone, his call confers on the pitch the property of being a strike, and he creates a new baseball fact. In the same way, says Sveinsdóttir, people confer on others the property of being a member of a social kind.

Sveinsdóttir points out that there's another way of thinking about social kinds. Take the social kind "female," for example—Sveinsdóttir follows Judith Butler in thinking that not only gender but sex itself is a social construction (Butler 1990). We could say about females that the presence of sex-typical genitalia, hormonal levels, chromosomes, and the like *constitutes* being female. This is John Searle's view of how social kinds are constructed (Searle 1997): on a constitutive view (to return to the baseball analogy), the ball's traveling a specified trajectory from pitcher to catcher within the context of the game simply *constitutes* a strike. But Sveinsdóttir is unhappy with that view, at least when it comes to baseball. If the baseball fact were constituted by the trajectory of the ball, then baseball would have gone the way of football, where the playback tape shows definitively whether the ball went out of bounds. But in baseball, the umpire's judgment "plays a fundamental role in the game,... including how the game progresses as well as the explanations people give of what happens on the field," and it seems odd to say that there are these baseball facts that play no role in the game (Sveinsdóttir 2012, 6). So, while she's willing to say that the ball's flight *grounds the conferral* of the property of being a strike, she doesn't believe it constitutes it.

It doesn't much matter for present purposes whether the umpire's call constitutes or confers the status of "strike" on the pitch, but when it comes to social kinds, the constitutive view does indeed seem unsatisfactory. There, recall, the idea would be that having certain sex-typical features constitutes being female. But as Sveinsdóttir points out, what matters socially about being female— whether you will be given a girl's name, for example—is not what you are, but what you *seem* to be. And the conferral account captures, in a way that the constitutive account doesn't, the epistemic nature of this seeming. You might, after all, have XY chromosomes and androgen insensitivity syndrome, which means your androgen receptors don't function properly and, among other things, you end up with feminized genitalia. You look exactly like any other baby girl, and the doctor who delivers you has no reason to run a genetic test on you, so after she announces to your parents, "It's a girl!"[1] she registers that fact on your birth certificate. And you *are* a girl and will later be a woman, even if you do have XY chromosomes.

---

1. If the doctor were to preserve a strict sex-gender distinction here, she'd tell your parents, "It's a female!" But, like most doctors, she follows the common practice of assuming that the baby's sex tracks her gender.

But social-kind conferral isn't as authoritarian as strike conferral is in baseball. In baseball, even if the ball wasn't actually in the strike zone, what the umpire says goes. With social kinds, by contrast, conferrals are made by many other people, and as they don't always agree, their conferrals can be contested. If a person is transgendered, for example, or his genitalia are sufficiently ambiguous to cause the doctor to make a wrong call, an initial conferral of "female" misfires and can cause deep unhappiness unless (or until) the person manages to gain membership in the sex and gender kinds with which he actually identifies. This can be difficult to do, as it requires uptake on the part of others, but that makes my point: there is no one authoritative person—not even the person whose identity is at stake—who does the conferring.

There are unstated but widely shared rules for who belongs to what social kind, and as we learn to talk, we learn not only what the names of these social kinds are but also the rules for applying them to specific people—the rules that govern the language games in which social kinds have a place. Like any other rule, the ones for conferring membership in a social kind can't be completely codified; they work the way they do against the background of common assumptions and shared understandings that form our way of life. In following them, we participate in the practice of conferral that creates the social facts about who is a member of what kind. One of the social kinds we learn earliest is probably gender, but white and black, Jewish and Christian, and able-bodied and disabled can also become early categories for us if we have a direct experience of these differences (for example, you are a black child in a predominantly white environment) and if they are important to those around us.

In arguing for a conferral account of social kinds, Sveinsdóttir takes herself to be supporting what Sally Haslanger (2003) has called a "debunking project." Sveinsdóttir explains that exposing the nature of a category or kind serves the political aim of fighting oppression because it reveals "the categorization and related arrangements as needing justification, when it had appeared that they simply were the product of nature, where a demand for justification was inappropriate" (Sveinsdóttir 2012, 3). But here, I think, she is mistaken. While it's certainly true that abusive power systems are epistemically rigged to make it seem as if certain groups of people are just naturally inferior, so that no explanation is needed for treating them that way, the thing that needs debunking here is not the claim that the privileges and burdens attaching to a social kind are simply the product of nature, but the thought that even if they *were* simply the product of nature, a demand for justification would be inappropriate.

We can always ask if the assignment of privileges and burdens is relevant to a natural fact. Suppose, for example, there was definitive proof that homosexuality is caused by the presence of a "gay gene." That fact alone would tell us nothing whatsoever about whether lesbians and gays should be permitted to marry, because the gender of the person to whom one is sexually attracted is no more relevant to her eligibility for marriage than how much she weighs or how many brothers and sisters she has. Or, to take another example, the natural fact that women are typically capable of gestation tells us nothing about who should be responsible for childcare—it simply has no bearing on the question.

Some natural facts are, of course, relevant to social assignments of privileges and burdens: if you are incapable of carrying a tune, you aren't entitled to sing in the church choir, and if you haven't the talent to pass the bar exams, you don't get to practice law. But even here, you can always ask if exclusion from the choir also unfairly excludes you from other desirable social circles or if the bar exams bear the right kind of relevance to the practice of the profession.

And you can ask who benefits from these exclusions. In short, the need to justify the norms for what people of a given kind must or may not do, and for how they may be treated, doesn't depend on whether the kind is conferred or constituted by natural properties within a given social practice, but on how relevant the properties are to the privileges or burdens in question.

Then what is the point of the conferral-constitution distinction? Well, on the conferral account, we are not always what we seem, but we will be treated according to who we seem to be, even if that's not who we are. This explains the viability of identities even when they misrepresent us. The stories by which I understand myself, for example, can falsely depict me as a social drinker who doesn't have a problem with alcohol; the stories then become a part of my self-conception, and I act on the basis of them. Similarly, the second- and third-person stories that enter my identity can misrepresent me, but I will nevertheless be treated according to that misrepresentation.

Sometimes these inaccurate portrayals are benign—you mistake me for a fellow Jew, say, or I am not as French as I think I am—but other times they are not. If the master narratives depicting my social kind portray me as lazy, dirty, slutty, and stupid, people with enough social power to benefit from seeing me that way are apt to treat me that way. In fact, the narratives purport to *justify* treating me that way. Additionally, my own consciousness may be infiltrated by those narratives, and then I will treat myself that way.

An identity damaged by the abusive social group relations that give rise to these demeaning stories can, on the conferral account, be *contested*. The identity can be rehabilitated by counterstories that represent the person in a more accurate and respectworthy light, but narrative repair is possible only if the counterstory gets taken up by the socially powerful groups who benefit the most from the oppressive social system (Nelson 2001). The conferral account is to be preferred, then, because identities can be tentative and corrigible, whereas truly constitutive properties are not. Constitution is infallible, but conferral is apt to misfire.

HOLDING IDENTITIES AND LETTING THEM GO

The master narratives that depict the social kinds of which we are members are only one type of story that contributes to a personal identity. Equally important are the personal stories that portray important acts and events in our lives, significant relationships, distinctive characteristics, and serious commitments. At first—in the construction of Ellie's identity, for example—these will be stories of relationship, narratives that portray Ellie as a member of *this* family, the daughter or niece or sister of *these* people. Soon, though, stories of Ellie's acts and experiences, such as the one about the day she and Jack-Jack got lost in the woods, enter into her identity as well.

Notice how Jack and Ellie learn to tell their own stories about their acts, experiences, and characteristics. Mama prompts Jack to tell a backward-looking story that will explain how he got his sweater so dirty. Ellie prompts Jack to remember that they saw a frog. These "stories of reminiscence" require children to weave their memories into a continuous narrative, but younger ones can only do it if older people explicitly mention the events at the time. It's not until children are five years old (Ellie is six) that they can produce complicated and original stories of what happened when, for example, they got lost in the woods (Nelson and Fivush 2004). Robyn Fivush and Katherine Nelson explain why these stories are important:

Although all children will develop autobiographical memories, children of more highly elaborative mothers will come to have more highly elaborated and coherent autobiographical memories than children of less elaborative mothers. Moreover, as children develop the language and narrative skills to organize and recall their past through participating in adult-guided reminiscing, they are also beginning to differentiate the past as past, that is, to understand time and sequence and how past experiences fit along a developing time line. Through locating past events in time, children begin to develop the idea of a continuous self, a self that exists through time. (Fivush and Nelson 2004, 575)

Elsewhere Fivush explains, "Families that are more elaborative, with each family member contributing to the ongoing narrative and sharing their perspectives and opinions, have children with higher levels of self-esteem and emotional well-being. More specifically, families that are able to reminisce about highly stressful events in an emotionally expressive and explanatory fashion have children with higher levels of self-understanding and self-esteem" (Fivush 2008). It seems, then, that the identity-constituting stories the child herself constructs do more than give the child a sense of herself as existing through time—they also teach the child how to value herself.

The personal part of the identity, like the part involving membership in social kinds, is conferred: what matters for practical purposes is who you appear to be (either to yourself or to others), not who you are. Again as with social kinds, the conferral is meant to track the underlying natural properties, but here as there, it doesn't always do so. Again, too, resistance is possible if the identity-constituting stories that misrepresent who one is can be exchanged for more accurate narrative representations and if the new stories get the appropriate uptake.

Just as families are primarily responsible for initially constructing the child's identity, so, too, are they primarily responsible for *holding* the child in it. They do this by treating him in accordance with their narrative sense of him, and in so doing, they reinforce those stories. But identity maintenance also involves *letting go*: weeding out the stories that no longer fit and constructing new ones that do. It's in endorsing, testing, refining, discarding, and adding stories, and then acting on the basis of that ongoing narrative work, that families do their part to maintain the child's identity.

As he grows, of course, the child contributes more and more to this process himself, as do his playmates, teachers, neighbors, and the others he encounters in his life. And just as important, these others challenge him, interrupt certain patterns of behavior, encourage self-transformations of various kinds, and help or force him to grow in particular directions (Kukla 2007). But when the new kid at daycare calls Jack names, when Ellie tells him he's adopted, when he has had a bad day—when, in short, his grip on himself is temporarily shaky—what he needs most is to be *held* in his identity. It is then that the adults in his immediate family have the special job of reminding him, by how they interact with him, of who he really is.

Even very young children can hold someone in her or his identity. A toddler just learning to talk, for example, might associate the grandmother he sees only infrequently with the song she sings to him when she comes to visit. Then, the next time she comes, he demands the song. His understanding of who she is may be limited, and *how* he holds her in her identity might be clumsy, but it's a genuine instance of holding all the same—he is maintaining her identity by engaging in the recognition and response that is part of the practice of personhood.

Whether master narrative or purely personal, the stories required to represent selves that are continually growing and changing run in two different directions, each with its attendant dangers. Some are backward-looking: they explain how the child got to be who she is. The story of Ellie and Jack in the woods is likely to dog her at family gatherings for years; it becomes, we'll suppose, a partial explanation of her feisty and fearless character. Or as a story of relationship, it might explain what good friends the brother and sister are.

The danger with backward-looking stories is that if family members don't let go of them when they no longer explain who the child is, they can keep the child from growing: if Jack is seen as easily led, Mama and Daddy might not allow him to go off on his own with Ellie anymore. If Ellie is seen as naughty and disobedient, Mama and Daddy might not let her out of their sight. Not letting go of outgrown stories unfairly constricts children's agency and diminishes their self-respect, and unless the children later manage to contest and repair the damage done to their identity, their lives can go badly for them. Should, to continue the example, Mama and Daddy deny Ellie opportunities to exercise self-reliance, she might find it difficult to make good decisions, which in turn could impair her confidence in her own abilities. In that way, her parents could make of her precisely the wayward, impulsive person they took her to be.

Other stories are forward-looking: they set the field of the child's future actions. One way they do this is by opening up the future, through identity-constituting stories that allow the child to explore many possible avenues for her particular talents and inclinations. Ellie says to Jack, "We can be explorers, and go exploring." Mama says to Ellie, "When you're older, you'll be a good speller just like Charlotte, only without the web." Or Ellie pretends that, like Hermione Granger, she is the best witch of her year.

The danger with forward-looking stories is that they can close down rather than opening up the person's options. Ellie sees movies and TV shows that depict girls as airheads, her first-grade teacher doesn't expect much of her in math and science, she reads books in which the smart girls aren't the popular girls, her classmates subject her to dumb blond jokes (this is a few years down the road), and so on. If narratives of this kind enter Ellie's identity, she might be a good student but not be recognized for it or encouraged to succeed. Or worse still, she might internalize the stories and stop trying, in which case she becomes the dumb blond the stories show her to be.

ACQUIRING MORAL AGENCY

Because identities are normatively prescriptive—they tell you what you are supposed to do and how others may, must, or mustn't treat you—they play a large role in our moral lives. So learning what their own and other people's identities require of them is a part of children's moral formation. In turn, initiating children into moral life is part of the larger process of socializing them, as social practices are infused with moral ones. When Sylvia is taught not to dump the cereal out of her bowl, she begins to learn both table manners and consideration for others. When Jack is taught not to grab Ellie's toy, he begins to learn both what property is and what respecting his sister involves.

At first, the connection between "how we do things" and morality is often made explicit: Mama says, "Jack, don't hit—that's *naughty.*" As children grow, though, they learn that moral judgments need not involve moral terms at all: Daddy only has to say "Ellie, you and Jack got lost," and Ellie understands that she is guilty of wrongdoing.

Sabina Lovibond gets a little help from Wittgenstein as she explains how this works. In his 1938 *Lectures and Conversations on Aesthetics, Psychology and Religious Belief*, Wittgenstein is reported to have said that "in real life, when aesthetic judgements are made, aesthetic adjectives such as 'beautiful,' 'fine' etc. play hardly any role at all.... The words you use are more akin to 'right' and 'correct.'" At the heart of Wittgenstein's observation, Lovibond says "we seem to see the paradigm of a conversation which *rests as lightly as possible on the surface* of the speakers' common understanding of effects to be achieved or avoided, and which proceeds by a series of moves calculated to call attention to just those points that may not be obvious... on this common basis" (Lovibond 2002, 39–40).

This phenomenon, as Lovibond points out, is not restricted to aesthetics, but can also be observed in conversations about ethics. She asks us to consider this schema: "Had you thought of just...?"—"Oh, I couldn't possibly do that"—"No, I suppose not." "The second speaker (*B*) offers no reason why the other's (*A's*) suggestion is unacceptable," says Lovibond. "Their common history of 'immersion' in a moral culture makes that superfluous. Nevertheless, the exchange is not useless for purposes of moral guidance since it leads *A* to manifest a view of her own suggestion... which, if sincere, gives *B* a certain very precise insight into the way *A* takes that culture to impinge on the problem at hand." Lovibond notes the quality of *intimacy* that characterizes conversations of this kind: much of what matters remains unspoken, because the conversation "proceeds against the background of an essentially shared evaluative environment" (Lovibond 2002, 42). Jack is still learning the commonly held moral understandings that operate in his world, but Ellie knows enough of them to make explicit references unnecessary. Her conversation with her father can rest lightly on the surface of their common understanding.

But what, exactly, was there for her to understand? In itself, getting lost wasn't wrong. Even getting lost because she left the playground wasn't wrong. Nor was her disobedience in leaving the playground. What was wrong was that she disobeyed *her father*, who has the authority to require her obedience. And the reason he has that authority is that he is responsible for his children's well-being until the children are old enough to take on this responsibility for themselves. Ellie and Jack aren't yet practiced enough at seeing the "shape" moral reasons take in a given situation to be able to make accurate moral judgments, so they have to rely on their parents' judgments. But none of that needs to be said when everyone understands it—it forms the background against which what *is* said makes sense. What Daddy says forces Ellie to confront what she did, and when she does that, she has to admit she shouldn't have done it.

From a very early age, then, children are moral agents. But much of their agency is exercised for them, as it were, by their parents, who make the appropriate moral judgments and teach the children to act accordingly, while the children's role is largely one of obedience. And as the children obey, they are drawn "into outward conformity with a linguistic practice" (Lovibond 2002, 84): they learn to say that *this* act, in this context, is "naughty"; *that* one, in that context, is "helpful"; and so on. Initially, this imitation is mere behavior; it's not yet a genuine expression of the child's own moral commitments. It's only the first step in what becomes a *"progression* toward authorship of the moral judgements of which one gives oneself out as author" (Lovibond 2002, 97).

The child, says Lovibond, is in something like the position of the drunken actor who, in the *Nicomachean Ethics*, spouts the verses of Empedocles—he says all the right things, but he doesn't fully know what he's saying. Rather than being the author of the words, the child is merely a mouthpiece for them (Lovibond 2002, 97–98). The judgments issue from his parents' standpoint, external to the child's own. As he grows, though, he develops the faculty for critical reflection that allows him to *endorse* the judgments—or repudiate them. Once he's capable of this, his judgments will be a more authentic expression of his personality, evincing dispositions that are more fully his. His attitude toward them will be, not one of parroting what his parents say, but of his own authorship.

What role do personal identities play in exercises of moral agency? For one thing, they factor largely in the practices of responsibility and accountability that constitute morality (Walker 1998). If *Jack* had told her to stay on the path, Ellie needn't have obeyed him, because he is just Jack-Jack and she is not accountable to him in that way. The wrong-making feature of leaving the path was the fact that *Daddy* told her not to—his identity as Daddy gives him that authority over her. Ellie is, of course, accountable to many other people as well: she has to obey Mama, her teacher, and her babysitter, and also her aunt, her uncle, and her grandparents, especially when her parents aren't around. Because she is Jack's sister, she is more responsible for his safety and well-being than are the other kids in the neighborhood; if they are mean to him, she is supposed to put a stop to it, and if he gets hurt, she's supposed to take him home. In fact, many of Ellie's "supposed to's" derive from either who she is or who someone else is with respect to her.

To explain another important role personal identities play in our moral lives, I need to take a little detour into the philosophical literature on free agency. According to Gerald Dworkin (1970), Harry Frankfurt (1988a), Wright Neely (1974), Gary Watson (1975), and Daniel Dennett (1984), there are two necessary conditions for free agency: the ability to act intentionally and the capacity to regulate one's will reflectively. In general, these theorists think that one has to be able to control one's conduct through deliberate choices that express what one really wants to do. So they typically say that young children aren't free agents. In fact, Frankfurt classifies children as "wantons," incapable of taking the higher order attitude toward their desires that he thinks is necessary for a well-controlled will.

As Paul Benson has suggested, insisting that a control condition is sufficient for free agency is a mistake that could only be made by philosophers who have never been a young child's primary caregiver. Who else would think that a five-year-old boy who has been warned not to tease his baby sister but does it anyway must be out of control, hopelessly driven by desires he can't help acting on? (Benson 1990, 52). Even three-year-old Jack-Jack can stop spitting into his milk when he sees it makes Mama mad. What he and Ellie *can't* yet do, though, is express who they are by what they do. Benson calls this "normative self-disclosure" and says the lack of it keeps a person from being fully free. The thrust of his article is to explain why women who don't conform to the sexist norms of their society aren't free—namely, that they will "typically assess some of their actions in ways which diverge from mainstream assessments," and this in turn "reduces their freedom in relation to mainstream perceptions of their conduct" (Benson 1990, 54).

I want to focus, though, on why *children* aren't free. As Benson has it, the reason is that they aren't capable of fully appreciating the standards by which others judge them, so how they act doesn't express who they are (Benson 1990, 53). But while Benson puts this in terms of what children don't yet appreciate, I think it's also a matter of *commitments* they aren't yet capable of. To hark back to Lovibond, they are in effect trying out, or playing at, the normative standards their parents have taught them, but they are too young to reflectively endorse what they do and so make their actions their own. They aren't yet fully the authors of their actions, and that is why what they do doesn't say very much about who they really are.

From Ellie's disobedience in leaving the playground, for example, we can't infer that she is a wayward child, given to headstrong behavior. That inference might be licensed if she were an adult and proud of her strong will, in which case the story of what happened in the woods when she was a little girl could still accurately depict something important about her. As it stands, though, all we can say is that the story *might* someday be one that accurately portrays her—but then again, it might just as easily not. With respect to the six-year-old Ellie's behavior, we can't infer anything much from that story. Only years later, after she's made repeated choices that reveal her commitment to having her own way, would we be entitled to make a judgment of that kind.

Of course, a one-time action doesn't usually say anything much about morally mature adults, either. That Jack and Ellie's parents got so caught up in their conversation with Uncle Eric and Aunt Lori as to lose track of their children constitutes carelessness, but the inference that they are careless parents isn't licensed unless this particular failure of attention is part of a pattern that shows they've adopted a laissez-faire approach to child rearing. The difference between the parents and Ellie is that the parents can have a momentary lapse in adhering to their own standard of conduct. Ellie can't do that yet, because the standards available to her aren't fully hers.

In short, because morality is something we do—and do together—it doesn't just set up normative expectations regarding who is responsible for what, or accountable to whom. It also *expresses* who we are in moral terms (Walker 1998, McKenna 2012). So, as children acquire moral agency, they not only have to get a feel for whose identity requires what response, but also have to become aware of what their actions say to others about who they are, in the knowledge that they will be treated accordingly.

As I hope I've shown, acquiring a second nature is a highly complex process. It requires children to engage with others in all kinds of language games, in the course of which they are brought into the space of reasons. They have to learn what words mean and the rules for using them correctly. They have to get the hang of the shared sensibilities that undergird rule following, rationality, and social life in general. They have to form a self-conception and a sense for who others are, both singly and together. They have to become storytellers. They have to appreciate the patterns of expression, recognition, and response in which their own and others' identities play a key role. They have to try on the moral values and attitudes they are taught and come either to question them or to claim them as fully their own. They have to act out of their sense of who they are and become aware that others will identify them by how they act.

And yet those two little kids who got lost in the woods one day have already got the hang of most of this. Astonishing, isn't it?

Chapter 4

Ordinary Identity-Work

How We Usually Go On

Our personhood is responsive, called into full expression
by other persons who treat us as one of them.

—Annette Baier

Someone—his host, maybe—put a beer in his hand and waved
him to the armchair by the fireplace, where he obediently sat
down. It was raining hard outside, but the front door had been
left open so the smokers could congregate on the porch, which
slightly relieved the overcrowding in the dimly lit living room. It
was an odd mix of people, he thought, peering into the assembly.
That one over there looked like a state senator, but the girl he was
talking to couldn't have been more than fifteen, and the truck-
driver type with his cap on backward had his arm around a young
man's waist.

"Hey, I'm Francine. I don't believe we've met?" A thirtyish
woman built on generous lines and displaying an impressive amount
of cleavage materialized in front of him.

"Bud Hewitt." He struggled to rise out of the overstuffed chair,
but she motioned him down and pulled up a nearby footstool.

"Are you Joel's daddy?" She sipped her cocktail, made a face, and set the glass on the carpet.

"That's right. You played Goneril, didn't you?"

"I did. The part's not so bad, except for dying on stage—I swear I've bruised my ass in a different place every single night of the run. Joel was great, though, wasn't he? Makes you wanna throw up when they gouge his eyes out."

Bud was beginning to enjoy himself. "Pretty realistic, all right." He took a sip of his beer. "What do you do when you're not doing— uh, this?" He waved his hand at the shadowy crowd, which was gradually getting noisier.

"State Farm Insurance like Joel, only in another department. I sort of got him the job. How about you?"

"I manage an electrical supply outlet in Memphis."

She widened her already wide, heavily made-up eyes. "Gracious. That's a long way to come to the theater."

"Well, I'm really here for a trade fair, but then Joel told me he was in the play, so I stayed on."

"All right for beer, Dad?" Joel lowered himself to the floor with a bump, a bottle in each hand. His face was flushed, and he spoke a little too carefully, as if he had already been enjoying more than his share of his host's hospitality. He looks like a friendly bulldog, thought Bud suddenly, but aloud he merely said he was fine.

"So what are you and Franny talking about?" Joel asked.

"About you, sweet boy." Francine helped herself to a satisfying swig of one of his beers and patted his stubbly cheek in thanks. "I was jes fixin' to ask your daddy how old you were when you caught the acting bug."

"You were in high school, weren't you, Son? I remember you being one of the Lost Boys in *Peter Pan*."

"That was my senior year, Dad. My first role was in eighth grade. I played the lead in *Brighton Beach Memoirs*."

"That's right, I forgot."

"Nothing new there," Joel muttered.

"Well anyway," Francine smiled brightly. "Great cast party. I've never been to Travis and Steve's before—have they lived here for long?"

"Well, they've been together for—oh, I guess about three years, which is when they got this place."

"It's real cute. Wasn't Steve the one whose parents kicked him out of the house when he told them he was gay?"

"Yeah, well, he was a little old to be living at home anyway. He just stayed there to save money while he was in school." Joel shrugged.

"Still, that's no way for parents to do." Bud set his beer down. "I mean, even if they didn't agree with his lifestyle, he's still their son."

"Sure," said Joel. "Instead of throwing him out, they could just pretend he doesn't exist. You could show 'em how to do that, couldn't you, Dad?"

Bud forced a smile. "Well, now, I reckon nobody's satisfied with how they were raised, are they, Miss Francine?"

"Just stop it, Joel," hissed Francine.

"No—it's interesting." Joel pulled at his beer and wiped his mouth with the back of his hand. "Tell her where you were on the opening night of *Inspector Hound*, Dad. Or *Streetcar*—that was a good one. Or how about the senior-year talent show? You were right there in the front row with Mom, clapping your hands off like you always did, right? Or no." He smacked his forehead. "I remember now—you were seeing clients, that's it!"

"I came when I could, Son."

"Sure you did. When I was in college, too. You were always there when I was doing the stuff that's important to me. I felt so affirmed.

Especially when you didn't bother to come to my honors thesis performance. That was the best."

"You *asshole*, Joel—shut up!" Francine was really angry.

"Don't believe I will. If I'd majored in business, now—well, you'd have liked that, wouldn't you, Dad? If I'd set my sights on something manly and important like working at a dead-end job where they don't even respect you, like you've done all your life?" He got unsteadily to his feet. "A toast!" he proclaimed loudly.

The noise in the room lessened as people turned to look. He gulped all that was left in the bottle and raised it high. "To the best dad any man could have. No—to more than that. To a beautiful human being and my all-time hero, Bud Hewitt!"

Francine laid her hand on Bud's arm. He patted it, smiled at her painfully, and stood up. Then, threading his way carefully through the assembly, he found his jacket and walked out into the rainy night.

THE PERFORMANCE

What must one do to hold someone in his identity? In this miniature interpersonal exchange, we see both morally good and morally bad holding, as well as good and bad letting go. The task of this chapter is to work out what makes identity-work go well or badly, but to do this, I'll first have to describe in greater detail just exactly how identity-work is done at all.

I've said that personhood is the practice of physically expressing one's personality to other persons who recognize the expression for what it is and respond accordingly. *What* one expresses is, cumulatively, one's own sense of who one is—it's one's personal identity, from the first-person perspective. And because identities are narrative constructions and narratives are always selective in what they depict, the expression is an edited one, meant to feature only those aspects of the self the person wishes to display in a particular setting.

It's an act, then, a kind of theatrical performance. Many parts of the performance are so thoroughly habitual that we don't notice them—performing gender, for example, is something we learn to do early, in the course of acquiring all the other elements of our second nature (Butler 1990). At other times, the performance is conscious and calculated, as when we are being interviewed for a job, trying to look good on a first date, or selling somebody something.

Just as a performance needs an actor, so, too, it needs a script. One part of the script consists of one or more of the socially shared master narratives that govern conduct in specific situations. So, for example, Daniel Kahnemann and Amos Tversky identify the "restaurant script," made up of rule-governed "entering," "ordering," "eating," and "exiting" scenes (in Nisbett and Ross 1980, 280). A visit to the grocery store, a phone conversation, an airplane journey, a children's play date, a cast party—these are all situations for which there are well-established scripts that show us what we are supposed to do in them. The second part of the script—the role the person is playing—consists of a selection from the tissue of stories that forms our self-conception. These scripts don't dictate the performance, of course. They're simply the stock plots and character types the actors make use of as they improvise the scene. When the actors play themselves improvisationally into the incompletely scripted situation, they collectively define that situation. It's not just any old cast party now, but a cast party in which these specific individuals have several legitimate roles: one of the actors is, let's say, both "Bud the guest" and "Joel's father."

A performance also requires an audience, which is to say that as we *express* ourselves, others will in turn have to be *impressed* by us in some way (Goffman 1959, 2). This is the "recognition" moment of personhood. When the audience consists of strangers, the social transaction proceeds solely by inference: I project a particular persona against the backdrop of a given situation, and the impression my performance leaves on you allows you to infer what kind of a person I am—the kind that decides not to behave courteously to my father at a party, for example. With colleagues, friends, and intimates, the promissory note left by my first impression has been repeatedly cashed in, so their sense of who I am, while still inferential, is richer and more detailed. This cumulative impression of me gives me a cushion of capital to draw on if I need it, in that if this evening I turn in a shabby performance, they can measure it against my earlier performances and decide whether tonight says something important about me or is just a one-off, attributable to illness, too much beer, or a bad day. I don't project the same persona to strangers and familiars equally, of course—I tailor my performance to suit my audience. I might, for instance, let my guard down with my dad and Francine, while showing my boss at State Farm how professional I am.

There's one more thing that the expression of an identity requires: other actors. Their job is to perform the "response" moment of personhood, which they do by taking up the dual role of audience and performer. As audience, they recognize your performance, but as actors, they project their own sense of themselves into the situation, where, if they are obeying the rules that govern these performances, they establish a surface consensus to the effect that yes, we are playing out the "cast party" script and yes, you are enacting the role of "guest" and so am I. In this way, they acknowledge you and help you uphold your definition of the scene. Erving Goffman sums it all up quite nicely:

> We have then a kind of interactional *modus vivendi*. Together the participants contribute to a single over-all definition of the situation which involves not so much a real agreement as to what

exists but rather a real agreement as to whose claims concerning what issues will be temporarily honored. Real agreement will also exist concerning the desirability of avoiding an open conflict of definitions of the situation. (Goffman 1959, 9–10)

A good analogy for all this is the commedia dell'arte, which flourished in Italy in the sixteenth and seventeenth centuries. The term means "comedy of the art," or "comedy of the profession," and refers to unwritten or improvised comic drama. The plots mostly revolved around clever tricks to get money or outwit a fool, disgraceful love affairs, and cases of mistaken identity, while the characters were the traditional "plotting maids, bragging captains, aged fathers, and wily widows" of New Greek and Roman comedy (Bellinger 1927, 154).

The commedia characters were well established: everybody knew Columbine, the saucy maid, and expected her to be in love with Harlequin, the acrobatic nuisance who carried a slapstick and whose rags later came to be stylized in a diamond pattern. They knew the pompous Doctor, who was never remotely competent at his profession, the swashbuckling but cowardly Captain, the greedy and stingy Pantaloon, the innocent and dreamy Pierrot, the malicious Punchinello or Punch, and the *innamorati*, or young lovers.

Audiences also knew how the stories would go—the *innamorati* would be thwarted by one or more of their parents but, with the help of Columbine or some other eccentric servant, would triumph in the end. There's also the one in which Harlequin becomes mysteriously pregnant, the one where a sneaky servant takes on two masters so he can make extra money, and the one where two brothers fall in love with the same woman. Occasionally, there's even a tragic ending.

It's because the characters and stories were so well known that the actors could improvise, heightening, varying, and embellishing their parts as their imagination and skill suggested. They had to find the right words to draw laughter or tears from the audience, the action had to move along smartly and smoothly yet be full of surprises, and they had to be ready for whatever their fellow actors threw at them and return the favor with wit and seeming ease. It required a great deal of talent, self-discipline, and practice on the part of the performers. No wonder, then, that it was the commedia dell'arte that introduced the professional actor into Europe (Bellinger 1927, 153).

Although we have all been playing improv, as it were, all of our lives, most of us aren't professionals, so we often perform our roles awkwardly. When the identity is one the rest of the cast has not had much experience with, the actor who bears it might have to engage in what has been called the "hidden labor" of manipulating the others into giving her the proper response. Jackie Leach Scully, who is hard of hearing, writes that when traveling, she has to "perform deafness"—for instance, by cupping her hand behind her ear and looking quizzical—if she's to convince flight attendants that she needs special notification of in-flight announcements (Scully 2010, 29). Because the stereotype about deafness portrays it as a complete loss of hearing, never a partial one, she has to exaggerate her disability. If she doesn't, the people whose help she needs are apt to suppose she can hear just fine.

Other forms of hidden labor that might help people with unusual or stigmatized identities to elicit the proper response include normalizing one's identity by downplaying the difference between it and everyone else's (we gay people don't think about sex any more than you do), parading the identity overtly so that it doesn't take the others by surprise (using a hook rather than an artificial hand), and passing for someone whose identity is socially acceptable (Franklin

Delano Roosevelt's refusing to be photographed in his wheelchair).
When skillfully executed, these techniques for managing others'
responses can keep the scene moving forward without any hitches,
though with possible loss to the person who is forced to engage in
this labor. When the identity is damaged (Nelson 2001) by preju-
dice against disabled people, racism, or other forms of bigotry, hidden labor can be necessary for survival.

The rules that govern the expression and uptake of an identity
are not just social but also moral: in the same way that stage actors
are meant to cover for each other when one of them drops a line or
in some other way stumbles in the performance, so in ordinary social
interchanges the participants are expected to help each other preserve the definition of the scene they have collaborated in establishing. They do this by responding appropriately to the personae being
projected, and in that way they hold the others in their identities. To
do so is called tact. To fail to do so is to humiliate one's fellow actor.

ON WHOSE AUTHORITY?

Where does the authority to perform an identity come from? The
social authority depends in part on how much social power you possess (Goffman 1959, 60). Those with high status have the authority
to claim not only their own identities but also identities of lower
status, because entitlement to behave like the masses is part of what
it is to enjoy social privilege: if you've ever picked up a gossip weekly
at the supermarket checkout counter and read a headline like "Star
buys her own groceries, takes son to the zoo!" you will see what
I mean. If you have a lower status, though, you don't get to enact a
higher class identity without incurring derision, dismissal, or out-
rage. "Who," others will think to themselves or say to your face,

"do you think you are?" If your identity is absolutely intolerable to those with more power, you may not be authorized to perform it at all: think of gays or transpeople in some contemporary U.S. circles, or Jews in Nazi Germany.

Goffman claims that the moral authority to perform an identity comes from its being properly your own: "Society is organized on the principle that any individual who possesses certain social characteristics has a moral right to expect that others will value and treat him in an appropriate way. Connected with this principle is a second, namely that an individual who implicitly or explicitly signifies that he has certain social characteristics ought in fact to be what he claims he is" (Goffman 1959, 13). There's something to this, of course, but it's only true in the ideal case. Goffman isn't really thinking about the broad social features of life that shape interpersonal encounters, especially the oppressive forces that run through every society. When a person whose identity is damaged by these forces can't be sure that others will value and treat him appropriately, he might have to perform an identity that isn't altogether genuine. Scully, as we saw, is morally entitled to perform the identity of a stereotypically deaf person to get the extra help she needs. It's also worth noting that, if the identity is an oppressively contested one, the person bearing it may have the moral authority to claim it, even though her oppressors don't recognize her right to it: a woman might be morally entitled to a management position in her firm despite the vice president's refusal to grant her the social authority to take up the job. And of course, stage or film actors are authorized by social convention to perform whatever identity they please.

The authority to bear some parts of one's identity is conferred even before birth—Francine is a Wilson, black, middle-class, Frank's firstborn. Other parts, such as "college graduate," have to be earned, while still others require other people to take up reciprocal identities—employee and employer, for example. Identities such as doctor or fraternity brother can ordinarily be bestowed only by those who are already authorized to bear them, while others, such as Nobel Prize winner or felon, are conferred by committee. Moreover, an identity can be more or less properly one's own. The fact that I stole a candy bar from the 7-Eleven makes me a thief, but I'm not as much of a thief as someone who embezzles millions of dollars from a pension fund. Similarly, someone who sketches still lifes for a hobby is authorized to call herself an artist, but she hasn't the same claim to that identity as does a full-time painter.

HOW THE PERFORMANCE GOES WRONG

If all this is roughly right as a picture of how identities are expressed and taken up by others, then we can see plainly enough that holding others in their identities is an integral part of the performance. But because holding typically involves a holder's responding improvisationally to what the person being held is doing, while at the same time the holder is performing her own identity and there are often other actors in the scene who must also be held in their identities, and, on top of that, the person being held might be doing something the holder didn't expect or doesn't know how to respond to—well, the act of holding can get so complicated that even a commedia actor could find herself in over her head. As identity-work takes place in each of the four moments of the practice of personhood, let's try to sort out the complications by considering how holding can go wrong at each of those moments. It's important to bear in mind that the moments are discrete only analytically; in practice, they are so interconnected that, as you'll see, they stay linked even as I try to discuss each one individually.

Malfunctioning Mental States

We begin with thoughts, feelings, intentions, and attitudes—the "soul" that Wittgenstein speaks of as expressed on the body. Consider young Joel Hewitt, in our opening story. The setting for the identity performances he, his father, and Francine are playing out is a cast party, where all three of them are guests and Francine and Bud Hewitt are strangers to each other. Bud's and Francine's performances of stranger-at-a-party can't be faulted: both project friendliness, a sense of the occasion, and a willingness to display something about who they are without committing the social sin of too much information. They play off each other—hold each other in their identities—using the "party" script and inserting themselves into that script in the right sort of way, finding things in common to talk about while letting a bit of their own personalities show.

Joel, however, is acting out a "family quarrel" script, refusing to protect Bud's projection of himself as a decent dad. Bud's performance exerts a claim on Joel: it's a moral demand that he be treated with the kind of respect that is one's father's due. In declining to collaborate with Bud in defining the scene, then, Joel *lets him go*, humiliating him by failing to hold him in an important and contextually relevant aspect of his identity. And he magnifies the humiliation by letting him go in front of a stranger.

Now, it's certainly possible that Bud is not authorized to perform the role he is playing: perhaps he has been an abusive or grossly neglectful parent. In that case, Joel might be justified in refusing to protect Bud's performance, though even then we can fault him for discomfiting Francine and the other guests in the highly public way he chooses to do it. But let's suppose that Bud is not a bad father. Then the likeliest explanation for Joel's letting go is that there is something amiss in Joel's mental state. Maybe he is just that kind of a guy: a narcissistic, angry young man who rides roughshod over social conventions and other people's feelings. In that case, he needs to get a grip and grow up—which is to say, he needs to weed out the defective stories that cross his own consciousness about who he is (particularly with respect to his father), because he has no business acting on those stories. Or maybe the trouble lies directly with his brain: perhaps, as seems most likely, he's drunk. Or perhaps he is brain injured. Possibly he has been taking steroids, and the anger is a side effect of the drug, or he suffers from a mental illness. Maybe he has been brainwashed or is in such pain that he can't think straight. Any such disordering of Joel's "soul" could be enough to cause this particular instance of holding to misfire.

If his mental state is indeed at the root of the trouble, then to the extent that Joel brought it on himself, he's morally culpable for his failure to hold his father. If, for example, he has deliberately nursed his resentments against Bud until they are magnified out of all proportion, then he not only wrongs his father now but has been doing so for some time and can be held responsible for that. If, on the other hand, the mental malfunction is something he can't control, he's not a fit candidate for blame, although we may hold him to account for previous actions he could have controlled—the number of beers he consumed, for instance—that have put him into the present state where he can't help himself. Whether culpable or not, if similar malfunctions can be expected in the future, the other actors may come to see him as a performance risk and exclude him from their repertory company (Goffman 1959, 91).

Misleading Expressions

The way others respond to us depends heavily—although not entirely—on what we reveal to them about who we are. The physical expression of an identity can involve anything from heroic deeds to Facebook updates, with modes of dress, body language, choice of vocabulary, room décor, and characteristic mannerisms falling somewhere in between. Sometimes there is a local code, a signal meant only for certain other people. For example, when the cast party's cohosts first met at an audition, Steve correctly interpreted the flipped-up collar of Travis's polo shirt to mean that he was gay.

Expressions of identity can go wrong in two ways. The first way is to deliberately deceive others by withholding something important about oneself. Again, consider Steve. All the way through high school and college, he kept his identity as a gay man hidden from his parents. When he finally came out to them, their disgust and contempt for him caused a permanent breach in the family, and they haven't seen or spoken to him for the last five years. When the price for expressing one's full identity comes at such a cost, this sort of deception seems understandable. Indeed, the fact that the identity is stigmatized excuses the secrecy, just as it does in cases of hidden labor, where, as we saw, it excuses exaggerating a disability to get the appropriate response. In other sorts of cases, though, withholding something important about who you are is morally impermissible. It may be acceptable when you are first getting to know someone, but if you withhold an important fact long enough, it becomes a lie. An office flirtation can be good clean fun, for instance, but at some point you need to let him know you are married, or you wrong both him and your husband. When your relationship with a woman is no longer casual, you may not suppress the fact that you have a child. And you certainly may not paper over the fact that you are withholding something important about yourself by assuming a false identity as a diversionary tactic—you may not, for example, conceal your lower-class origins by hinting of your socially privileged childhood.

This brings us to the second way in which expressions of identity go wrong: deliberately deceiving others by performing an identity to which one isn't entitled. Think of the confidence artist, the charlatan, the impostor. Under ordinary circumstances, wholesale deceptions of this kind are morally forbidden, although exceptions might include wartime spying, disguising oneself to escape an enemy, or entering a witness protection program. Complete self-reinvention, in the manner of Jay Gatsby, is an understandable American fantasy but arguably morally dubious, because others are ordinarily entitled to count on you to be who you say you are. More common, perhaps, are performances that are only partly misleading. On a first date, for example, you might express more enthusiasm for the opera than you really feel, because you find out she's a devotee. While that's a pretty mild offense, a more culpable partial deception would be to offer a prospective employer false credentials or to practice medicine without a license. Extramarital affairs are also cases of deliberate deception, but here the wrong is compounded by the fact that the person you are deceiving has special reason to trust you to be the faithful spouse you pretend to be.

If deliberately withheld or flat-out false expressions of one's identity interfere with proper holding, so does a seriously distorted self-conception. If the stories that constitute my identity from the first-person perspective are blatantly inaccurate, others won't even try to hold me in it—their refusals will range from good-natured teasing to making fun of me behind my back, angrily demanding that I stop, putting me in the care of a psychiatrist, or calling the police, depending on just exactly who I take myself to be. Subtler inaccuracies may still allow others to coordinate their performances to mine, but they will only be able to hold me as well as my enactment allows (think of the person who is passed over for promotion because she consistently underplays her achievements).

There is one final thing that impedes the expressions required for good holding: immobilization or confinement of the person's body. This can be inadvertent, as, for instance, when injury or illness induces paralysis or a natural disaster strikes and one is buried under the rubble. But many of the means used for immobilizing someone are socially constructed or done on purpose: Botox injections, social conventions that dictate tight skirts and high-heeled shoes, house arrest, imprisonment, intentional maiming, war. Analogous to these are the virtual confinements produced by censorship, the necessity for closeting oneself, confiscation of one's passport so that one cannot travel, and removal of one's phone or Internet access. When who you are can't be expressed physically, others may still be able to hold you somewhat generically in personhood, but they will find it difficult or even impossible to hold you in your personal identity.

Misfiring Recognition

The most common reason by far for failures to hold someone in her identity is that the stories by which others recognize him are defective. Where the identity-constituting stories are master narratives that portray the social group to which the person belongs as morally inferior, the damage to the person's identity can be considerable. Because identities function as guides to the treatment of those who bear them, a person whose identity has been damaged can be prevented by those with greater social power from fully exercising her moral agency or enjoying access to the goods that are on offer in her society.

Charles Taylor puts it this way: "Nonrecognition or misrecognition can inflict harm, can be a form of oppression, imprisoning someone in a false, distorted, and reduced mode of being" (Taylor

1992, 25). Taylor argues, though, that the demand for recognition, whether in the "intimate sphere" or the "public sphere," is a modern invention, based on an ideal of authenticity in which each of us is bidden to be true to ourselves and our own particular, highly individual ways of being. He contrasts this with an older understanding of selves as socially derived, where recognition was based on social categories that everyone took for granted. "In premodern times, people didn't speak of 'identity' and 'recognition'—not because people didn't have (what we call) identities, or because these didn't depend on recognition, but rather because these were then too unproblematic to be thematized as such" (Taylor 1992, 35).

His point is that in modernity, the "inwardly derived, personal, original identity" has to *win* recognition and the attempt can fail, whereas in earlier times general recognition was enjoyed a priori, because based on social categories everyone took for granted. But I wonder if Taylor is right about this. It's one thing to say that recognition used to be a function of social status—one was seen as occupying a particular station in life and treated accordingly. It's quite another to say that it's only the shift to a more individualistic view of the self that renders that recognition problematic. The recognition extended by those in power in medieval Europe to slaves, serfs, servants, people with disabilities, poor people, women, and outsiders such as Romani and Jews confined those groups to highly specific spheres of social activity and was withheld if members of those groups attempted to venture outside their assigned spheres. The picture was one of a Great Chain of Being, featuring God at the top and a hierarchy of creation below him, with each person knowing where she or he stood in the (God-ordained) chain. That may have been unproblematic for the ruling classes, but it's just not true that the inferior social orders didn't have to strive for recognition. It's not only that they got none if they ventured outside the station in which God set them—one mark of their social inferiority was precisely that, *within* those stations, they were to make themselves as invisible as possible. Servants were supposed to efface themselves, women were not to occupy the pulpit or any other public speaking place, and Jews were to stay in their ghettos. Indeed, this invisibility was sometimes a matter of literal survival: until about 1830, it was perfectly legal in many parts of what is now Germany to hunt the Romani for sport (Trumpener 1995, 357). It's hard to see this sort of thing as anything other than a morally reprehensible, deliberately engineered failure of recognition.

Taylor goes on to point out that the reason for altering the curricula of secondary schools and universities to make a place for women and for men of non-European cultures is to give due recognition to groups that have traditionally been excluded. Because "dominant groups tend to entrench their hegemony by inculcating an image of inferiority in the subjugated, the struggle for freedom and equality must...pass through a revision of these images" (Taylor 1992, 65–66). To revert to my own vocabulary, the revised curricula offer counterstories that, if taken up by the socially powerful, can repair the damaged identities and so free the agency of the people who bear them.

Sometimes lack of recognition is encouraged for reasons of state. Consider, for example, how soldiers are trained to withhold recognition of the "souls" depicted on the bodies of their enemies. They shoot at silhouettes in the shape of human beings, learning to see that shape as a target rather than as a person. They play violent video games that increase their skill in blowing up, smashing, or stabbing the human form. They engage in unscripted field exercises that involve hunting down actual human beings who must pretend to die if they are caught. Shortly after the September 11 attacks, ABC News reported on a new simulator game for infantry training. "Soldiers take up position in front of a large screen depicting a desert hillside in Afghanistan. Tiny figures emerge from the dunes at a simulated distance of 1,000 feet. As they get closer, they become recognizable as Taliban fighters. Using standard M16 rifles equipped with laser points rather than bullets, the soldiers target the Taliban fighters" (ABC News 2001).

Weaponry functions to withhold recognition as well. When Henry V's English and Welsh forces triumphed decisively over the French at the Battle of Agincourt because his archers were armed with longbows, there was an outcry to the effect that it was cowardly to kill a man from so far away that one couldn't look him in the face. The use of airplanes to drop bombs from great heights has certainly exacerbated this complaint. Missiles, torpedoes, drones, tanks, and land mines also render the enemy faceless. And consider the euphemisms that withhold recognition of the real persons who are actually maimed or killed in war: it's a long list of words, but among them are "antipersonnel bombs," "civilian casualties," "fatalities," "friendly fire," and "collateral damage."

Failures of recognition occur commonly enough for personal reasons, too. A case of what appears to be morally bad holding is that of Terri Schiavo, whose parents insisted, despite her diagnosis of complete upper brain death, that she was awake and aware. Their refusal to let her go provoked an acrimonious and prolonged legal tussle that hurt all the parties involved save Schiavo herself. According to the *New York Times*, "The question of whether Ms. Schiavo should have been allowed to die, as her husband said she wanted, or be turned over to the care of her parents, who wanted to keep her alive, went on for seven years, and reached the Vatican, the White House, Congress and various state and federal courts, before finally reaching the Supreme Court, which declined to hear her case" (Williams 2005). Because they could not accept that she was in a persistent vegetative state, Schiavo's parents tried by every legal means possible to require her caregivers to continue administering artificial nutrition and hydration, over the objection of her formally appointed proxy decision maker—her husband—who wanted to stop what he regarded as futile care. The parents, holding Schiavo in an identity that depicted her as responsive and present to them, albeit severely impaired, were also holding her in her life, believing that she had an interest in maintaining it and in experiencing their loving care. Schiavo's husband, Michael, after many years of seeing her as his severely disabled wife, finally let go of her life, reidentifying her as someone whose brain was so damaged that she could have no interests of any kind, save the interest all human beings have in having important wishes honored and their bodies treated respectfully. The case caused a nationwide furor, but the husband prevailed, and she died thirteen days after the feeding tube that was keeping her alive had been removed.

The autopsy vindicated Michael Schiavo's letting go. It revealed that "Schiavo's brain had withered to half the normal size since her collapse in 1990 and that no treatment could have remotely improved her condition" (Goodenough 2005), in effect confirming the earlier clinical diagnosis of persistent vegetative state. In the absence of any upper-brain function, there can be no thinking or feeling, no sort of personality that could receive physical expression. For that reason, Schiavo, unlike my sister Carla, couldn't be held in personhood, and while there were still ways of holding her in her former identity, as I'll explain later, it couldn't be done in the way her parents were trying to do it.

Less devastating forms of morally bad holding can occur, as we have seen, when children grow out of earlier phases of their identities but their relatives or friends haven't yet caught up with the changes in who they now are. Family members in particular seem to have trouble weeding out old identity-constituting stories that no longer represent the person. If, when you were three, you got hold of the car keys and unlocked the steering column so that the car rolled down the driveway and crashed into a tree, you will forever be labeled (at least, by relatives who only see you once a year) as That Kind of Kid. Or if you have been a stay-at-home mom for many years but have now joined the paid workforce, the entire household may find it hard not to take it for granted that you will continue to keep hot meals on the table and clean socks in the drawer.

Innocently misfired recognition is possible, too. You might not realize that a business acquaintance has recently been widowed and so fail to read the lines on her face as inconsolable grief; you cannot then hold her in her identity.[1] Or you might, like Jane Austen's Emma, innocently withhold recognition from Jane Fairfax and Frank Churchill because you lack the important identity-constituting story of their secret engagement. In a rather different sort of case, you might fail to hold someone in his identity because you unwittingly missed your cue: you have every reason to think he and you are playing out the "office coworker" script, but he has fallen passionately in love with you and sees you as the Roxane to his Cyrano de Bergerac.

Sometimes lack of recognition is produced by social isolation. A person who is hard of hearing or visually impaired may have trouble picking up on what is being expressed. Literal isolation—solitary confinement, for example, or quarantine, or living in a sparsely populated area—can impede recognition, too. In these sorts of cases, it may be morally incumbent on others to make it possible for the person to engage in recognition. Sign language, audio

---

1. Other eras were kinder, facilitating recognition via widows' weeds or mourning bands that publicly proclaimed one's recent bereavement.

cues, visiting prisoners and shut-ins, keeping the roads plowed, and providing Internet access are important means of keeping people connected; a robust portion of that connection is the act of giving others uptake.

Misshapen Response

Oppressive master narratives that enter into social group identities commonly make it impossible for the people bearing those identities to express themselves adequately, and then, of course, what they say and do won't get the right kind of response. It's not that people in the stigmatized group can't utter the words or perform the actions that reveal their mental states, but that their oppressors refuse to acknowledge their right to have those states. The woman's No translates as playing hard to get, is taken as meaningless noise, or enhances the sense of conquest. The slave's "Leave him alone!" to the overseer goes altogether unheard or is punished as insubordination. The black teenager's hoodie gets registered as gang membership and the self-appointed neighborhood watchman shoots to kill. This kind of failure isn't only a failure of identity. It requires the cooperation of all sorts of oppressive social practices and material conditions—think of the great many things that would have had to be the case to make it possible for William Shakespeare's sister, always supposing he had one, to express her own literary genius (Woolf 2000)—but the defective identity-constituting stories purport to justify the group's ill treatment and in that way uphold the oppressive social order.

Note that the problem for the woman, the slave, and the teenager is not that they weren't properly recognized. Their oppressors certainly saw that they were a woman, a slave, and a teenager. In fact, it's likely that the rapist got off on knowing that she was a woman, and similar knowledge may well have heightened the titillation the overseer and the watchman got from abusing their victims. No, in all these cases, the problem is that the *response* was badly out of keeping with who these people are.

Defective responses between oppressive and oppressed social groups range from flatly atrocious to mildly disappointing. Atrocities such as mass extermination, torture, enslavement, and rape as a weapon of war are obvious examples of evil responses to who someone is. Segregation, lack of access to decent employment or education, high rates of incarceration, and civic disenfranchisement can't be classified as atrocities but are still despicable (Card 2005). And most insidious, perhaps, because subtle and quite difficult to uproot, are hostility and other negative attitudes toward members of a group, especially if they are attitudes the oppressor believes she does not have.

Defective interpersonal responses likewise fall on a continuum from horrific to slightly subpar. The obvious ones—murder, gross betrayal by someone you had special reason to trust, sexual violence—don't need further enumeration, nor do the lesser ones that we've all experienced in some form or another. It is perhaps not usual to think of the sarcastic remark your wife flings at you on her way out the door as an assault on your identity, but arguably it is: she has momentarily let go of her sense of who you are. As for tiny slights or a lack of response when, strictly speaking, none is called for, these are a normal part of the practice of personhood, and most of us can inure ourselves to them.

Occasionally, a misshapen response can be a morally good thing. Michael Walzer recounts a story George Orwell told about an incident that occurred when he was fighting against the Fascists in the Spanish Civil War. Orwell was in an air raid in which an enemy soldier, presumably carrying a message to an officer, jumped out of a trench and ran along the top of a parapet, half-dressed and holding up his trousers with both hands as he ran. Rather than do his duty and shoot the man, he let him go. Orwell wrote, "I had come here to shoot at 'Fascists'; but a man who is holding up his trousers isn't a 'Fascist,' he is visibly a fellow-creature, similar to yourself, and you don't feel like shooting at him" (Walzer 2006, 140). Of course, Orwell could see perfectly well that the man was a Fascist and an enemy soldier. There was nothing wrong with his eyes, either literally or figuratively. But he didn't respond the way one is supposed to when one is a soldier on active duty, because a man with his pants down just didn't strike him as the right kind of target.

A situation can actually *call* for a misshapen response. Had Francine, for example, simply stuck to her role of guest at a cast party by resolutely ignoring the family drama Joel was trying to establish, she would have been abetting his bad behavior instead of calling him on it. Had Bud, out of misplaced devotion to his son, accepted the public rebuke and offered an apology, he would have let go of his own identity and likewise abetted Joel's bad behavior. Neither of them was willing to hold Joel in his self-imposed role of injured son. As a general rule, this way of letting someone go is the correct response to an unauthorized performance.

WHEN MUST WE HOLD?

It appears, then, that where identities are concerned, there can be good letting go as well as good holding. But that brings us back to an earlier question: when are we morally obligated to hold? To answer that question, another spot of normative theory is in order.

In a recent paper, Margaret Olivia Little and Coleen Macnamara usefully distinguish among three kinds of force exerted by people's calls on one another (Little and Macnamara n.d.). Moral obligations carry *imperatival* force. They represent what we must do, not in any all-things-considered way, or weighing the merits for and against, but because not doing them is just flat against the rules. "Don't kill," "keep your promises," and the like are demands that, at least under privileged conditions, are moral requirements.

Not all deontic directives are requirements, however. Where a call on us carries *prescriptive* force, talk of "demands" seems out of place, and the more apt locution is something like "requests." Little and Macnamara offer three types of examples: my friend has been very good to me when I was ill and now asks a small favor; my brother needs a kidney and I am a suitable match; I've grabbed the last double seat on a crowded train and spread out my papers, but an elderly couple approaches and asks if I would mind moving to a nearby single so they can sit together. In none of these cases is the person entitled to *demand* that I comply, much less to make me do it. The most they can do is ask, and I have a right to refuse. Nevertheless, my refusal to help in these particular instances might be morally wrong.

To explain why, we need the third distinction. In each of the three examples, there is someone in need, and needs exert *commendatory* force. This is the weakest of the three forces; to meet the need is morally permissible and, indeed, might be an excellent thing to do. But there are a great many excellent things to do in this life, and we can't do all of them. So commendatory force isn't deontic. Need alone doesn't exert a strong enough pull.

What boosts the requests in the three examples up into the prescriptive range, according to Little and Macnamara, is a combination of the merits of the request and your relationship to the requester. "That your friend has helped you numerous times in the past; that he is your beloved brother; that you are the only one that could easily solve this problem. These are the features that here turn what would otherwise be commendatory force into prescriptive force for you" (Little and Macnamara n.d., 49–50). Another feature the authors don't consider but that could also exert prescriptive force is your own self-conception (Frankfurt 1988b, 91). "I have to accede to the request," you might feel. "I couldn't be me and do otherwise." The strength of this feeling will vary with the importance of the request; if you refuse to give up your seat to the elderly couple, you might feel only a mild sense that you had acted out of character, while refusing to give the kidney might leave you feeling altogether alienated from yourself—you feel the pull on you as a kind of necessity. However that may be, and however many its sources, the moral force is a personal one, not universally binding.

The difference between imperatival and prescriptive force can be measured by the aptness of *gratitude*: if I owe you obedience or respect or the truth, no thanks are in order; if I do you a favor or give you my kidney, they are—even if it would be wrong of me to refuse you. Other people have a right to turn you down, and indeed, it might be very odd of you to ask them. But because I stand in a special relationship to you, I may well feel your request is binding on *me*. I say "may" here, because there might be exculpatory considerations at play; my having three little children to care for might make a kidney donation too much of a risk, for example. That a justification of this kind is necessary, though, simply makes the point: in its absence, my refusal would be wrong.

Now, identities certainly make calls on us. As I've noted before, they give rise to normative expectations that mature moral agents ordinarily know how to meet. So one way to put the "When must we hold?" question is to ask whether these expectations ever exert imperatival force. And because holding others in specific identities rests on the more fundamental practice of holding them in personhood, we return to the question we first raised in chapter 1, of whether holding in personhood exerts imperatival force.

Not everyone taking human form *can* be held in personhood, of course. Corpses cannot, and nor, as we've just seen, can people in the true persistent vegetative state. They, like anencephalic babies, haven't enough brain function to support any kind of consciousness that could be given physical expression, so there is nothing there to recognize, and no response is possible. It seems to me, however, that under ordinary, privileged circumstances—when the person isn't suffering unbearably and untreatably, for example, or facing some other fate that is worse than death—those who can be held in personhood must be so held by the other persons with whom they interact. Letting them go casts them out of social and moral life, and to live outside that is to have no kind of human life at all. If the inability to have a life as a person is to have no kind of human life, and we have a right to life, it would seem we have a right to a human life—a life sustained by many kinds of relationships with other persons who look to us for sustenance as well. If we've a right to that, then the requirement to hold other persons in personhood shares its justification with the requirement not to murder, and is equally stringent.

It could be objected, along the lines of the famous Judith Jarvis Thomson argument, that even if a right to life as a person could be established, that doesn't yet establish your right to my services in holding you in it (Thomson 1971). All it would seem to establish is that I may not do anything—remove your cerebral cortex, for instance—that keeps you from holding yourself there. Most calls on people that carry imperatival force require us to *refrain* from acting, and in any case, all rights have boundaries, as the dictum about the right to swing my arm reminds us.

One problem with the Thomson-style objection is that there are plenty of positive calls on us that carry imperatival force, ranging all the way from the obligation to rescue the infamous toddler drowning in the shallow pond, to the duty to respond to an invitation. (Little and Macnamara think an RSVP is literally a request and therefore prescriptive, but I beg to differ. The proper reactive attitude on the part of the host isn't gratitude if you reply, but annoyance if you don't.)

The better reason to see holding in personhood as imperatival, though, is that a human life, to borrow Michael Bratman's lovely phrase, is a shared cooperative activity, characterized by mutual responsiveness, commitment to the joint activity, and—this is the crucial bit for present purposes—commitment to mutual support (Bratman 1992, 328). If we're playing basketball, to use one of Bratman's examples, and you're on the team, then the rest of us players have to pass the ball to you, set picks for you, and do all the other things teammates are supposed to do during the game. By the same token, if your life as a human being depends on your entering the practice of personhood and you have a right to life as a human being, then the rest of us in the practice have to commit to keeping you playing with us. After all, holding someone needn't take much effort: unless you stand in a special relationship to the person, eye contact, a smile, or a nod of recognition might be all that is required. Because the stakes for that person can be so huge and the claim on you is so small, it seems as if there is indeed an obligation to engage in this kind of holding. We'll have to revisit this question one more time in the next chapter, though, as an objection arises there that we haven't considered yet.

As to when the call to hold someone in a *particular* identity exerts imperatival force, my catalogue of ways in which holding can go wrong (which is hardly exhaustive) suggests that a great many considerations might have to be weighed in a judgment of this sort. Certainly, it seems as if the better you know someone, the greater the likelihood will be that certain ways of holding are demanded of you. The reason, in part, is that the relationship itself sets up normative expectations, as do the roles (friend, employee, father, coach) that may attach to it. But the scene you are acting out plays a part here as well. Your husband won't thank you if you hold him in that identity by straightening his tie in the middle of his presidential address; you were meant to be performing a rather different script that, at most, calls for you to stop fidgeting and assume an expression of fond devotion. And if a person is outgrowing a particular part of her identity, then even if you are right, strictly speaking, to hold her in it, it may be unseemly to do so.

HOW WELL MUST WE HOLD?

If there can be morally good and bad holding, there can also be excellent, poorly executed, and clumsy holding. No one is capable of uniform excellence—there are too many people in our lives and too many other calls on our time and attention. The best that most of us can do is hold excellently when our minds are on the job, which is more likely to happen, perhaps, when some person's or group's special need to be held focuses our attention. At those times, excellent holding may take on prescriptive force for us.

An example: suppose you are a successful professional in your mid-fifties and one day your boss, whom you've always liked, tells you the current economy forces him to lay you off. You learn that you are the only employee at your rank to lose your job and that your boss has just hired two junior replacements. You are deeply humiliated; the greater part of how you see yourself is tied up in your work, and you feel devastatingly betrayed by this man's letting go of your identity as the vice president for marketing. That evening, a close friend comes to see you, bringing with her a good bottle of wine and a copy of your résumé. She fills your glass and reads the résumé to you, item by item. Here is tact personified. As your identity has just suffered a real blow and you've temporarily lost your hold on it, she holds it for you, creatively and well.

A rather different kind of example: on January 29, 2012, Stacey Campfield, a Tennessee state senator who sponsored a bill that forbids homosexuality to be discussed in the public schools, walked into a restaurant in downtown Knoxville to have Sunday brunch with three friends. A few days earlier, he had made national headlines when, during a radio interview, he blamed the AIDS virus on a gay airline pilot's having sex with monkeys, adding that it was "virtually impossible" to contract the disease via heterosexual intercourse. When the owner of the restaurant, Martha Boggs, saw him coming in the door, she ordered him out, in no uncertain terms. As she told the press later that day, "It's just my way to show support for the gay community and stand up to somebody I think is a bully. He's really gone from being stupid to dangerous. I think he needs to know what it feels like to be discriminated against." The next morning, the sign in front of the restaurant read, "Today's Special: Fried Chicken. Crispy Chicken Livers. No Stacey" (Lakin 2012).

While not everyone has the opportunity to act in quite so public a manner, what Boggs did that Sunday was an admirable job of both holding and letting go. In refusing to play out the "restaurant" script with a bigoted actor attempting to play the VIP, she held gays and lesbians everywhere in their identity. Note that the call to do what she did was indeed prescriptive: she had a right to seat him, after all, though she refused to exercise it. Her action also passed the gratitude test—the *Huffington Post* reported that people from as far away as Switzerland and Thailand expressed their thanks on the restaurant's Facebook page (Signorile 2012). Many Knoxville citizens likewise expressed their thanks, making a point of eating at the restaurant as a way of showing appreciation.

Holding individuals or groups in their identities typically involves a sequence of many acts of recognition and response, over an extended period of time. Poorly executed holding refers to a specific instance or set of instances in that sequence that culpably fall below the minimum amount of care needed to do the job properly. You let yourself get so drunk at a cast party that you insult your father in front of all the guests. You immerse yourself so deeply in your job that you neglect your wife and kids. You keep putting off the visit to your elderly friend, even though you know she can't get out much anymore. Or you just lose your temper at a coworker and say nasty things you don't really mean. Poorly executed holding differs from culpable refusals to hold altogether in that you're holding where you should, all right—you're just doing it really badly.

Clumsy holding is different from this. The best way to explain it, perhaps, is with another story. Your great-aunt suffers from Alzheimer's disease, and her urinary incontinence finally convinced you that you could no longer care for her at her home, so for the past six months she's lived in a nursing home. Being uprooted from the place where she's lived for the last forty-odd years has greatly exacerbated her confusion. You go to see her several times a week, but you can never be sure she'll know you who you are. Sometimes she calls you by your mother's name; once she thought you were her sister, now long dead. Today she is having a good day, and her smile of recognition lights up the room. She calls you her little love and nods happily when you show her the pictures of your daughter's swimming meet. Near the end of the visit, she asks for her own photo album—she can't find the right term and finally calls it her picture book—and you climb up on a chair to pull it off the top shelf of the closet. Then she says, "You surely are a kind person. Kind and sweet. Are you here to see a relative?" Your heart breaks a little further, but you don't try to correct her. You just give her a hug and tell her you'll see her next week.

This woman holds her great-niece not well but clumsily, out of a fragmented and chaotic self-concept and an equally chaotic narrative understanding of who she is. Her grip—on the niece, on herself, on reality—is wobbly and unsure, yet for all its clumsiness, it's morally beautiful. It doesn't matter that she is no longer capable of rational reflection or of understanding her own situation. It doesn't even matter that she is no longer clear about whose identity, exactly, she is maintaining. Those considerations keep her from being able to hold well, but they don't stop her from holding clumsily. It is enough that she places this visitor somewhere in the vicinity of her great-niece, so that although her stories have disintegrated and her words have begun to fail her, the holding still goes more or less where she intends.

Toddlers, too, are capable of clumsy holding. Think of the woman whose two-year-old brings her a Band-Aid when she bursts into tears after a horrible day at work. The many little blows she sustained that day to her sense of who she is can't literally be repaired with a Band-Aid, but the toddler sees that something needs mending, and his deed actually does help her get a better grip on herself. If it comes to that, even infants, by breaking into a grin and stretching out their arms, can do their small part to hold their caregivers in their identities.

Nor is this clumsiness confined to persons who are not yet, or are no longer, capable of moral agency. Full-fledged moral actors are routinely clumsy, too, though perhaps not quite so strikingly. There's the joke you make at a party that falls flat and ends up insulting the person you were attempting to amuse. You are caught up in your own thoughts and walk down the street past a neighbor without speaking. Or you're in the awkward moment when a close friend has just thoroughly embarrassed herself and you haven't any idea how to rescue the situation.

Excellent, poorly executed, and clumsy holding; not bothering to hold when it's required; refusing to let go when it's time; culpable failures in any of the four moments of personhood—all this is the roughest sketch of an underexplored moral terrain. In this chapter, we've devoted most of our attention to comparatively ordinary, everyday interchanges among reasonably competent moral agents. In the next chapter, we'll take a closer look at the ethics of more demanding forms of holding.

Chapter 5

Struggling to Catch Up

Challenges to Identity-Work

What we notice in stories is the nearness of the wound to the gift.

—Jeanette Winterson

As he let her into the kitchen she'd known all her life, Papa's eyes were too bright—as if at any moment they might spill over with excitement or anger or some third uneasy thing. Emily set the groceries down on the counter and took off her coat, watching him warily as he put the food away. He didn't let her help with this because he wanted to show her that he could still do it by himself, so she sat down at the table and told him Sonja sent her love.

"Sonja?" He lurched from cupboard to counter to refrigerator, not with the old competence but clumsily, too fast for his brittle legs.

"My wife, Papa. She would have come with me tonight but she's stuck at the office. She's got a big sales meeting tomorrow and—"

"I know who you're talking about and I don't want her coming around here anymore," he interrupted. "She's a thief, that one. She steals from me. First she stole my—" he stopped, groping for the word—"my silver engine starter." He looked puzzled, but plowed on. "And then she stole my car, but she won't get any of my money, that's for sure. That's hidden someplace she'll never find it."

Emily had heard him talk like this before, but it still made her sad. "Oh Papa. Sonja didn't steal your car. We sold it for you last month, after the doctor told you it wasn't safe for you to drive anymore. Don't you remember?"

He shut the refrigerator door and turned to face her, jerking sideways to the nearest chair as if he preferred to keep the table between them. "What did you do with the money?" he demanded.

"It's in the bank." Sometimes if she used a sing-song tone she could keep him calm. "You got in my car and we went for a ride. We drove to the bank, all the way downtown."

The old man sat down, his back stiff and his mouth a thin tight line. It was a look she had seen sometimes in childhood, when he fought with her mother about money. Their fights terrified Emily and her brother, possibly because they happened so seldom. The children would sit at that very table, the gravy congealing on their plates, while Mama raged at Papa for his miserliness and he slammed his fist down so forcefully the plates jumped. At those moments, the children got a glimpse of something hard inside him that was usually buried deep under many layers of kindness. A splinter of cruelty that his disintegrating self could no longer conceal.

"Papa," she said desperately, "have you had your supper yet?" She had tried diversionary tactics before, and they sometimes worked. They worked now. He had been waiting for the groceries, he said, and yes, an omelet would be nice. She sautéed onions and mushrooms, made tea, buttered toast, folded the omelet. As she cooked, she teased him. "Do you even know which end of the can to open?"

Papa broke into a grin. "Of course not. But as your Grandpa David used to say, you don't have to know how to cook if your wife will do it for you."

"Yeah, right," she agreed. "Best guide for living that never actually applied to me."

"Applied to Sonja, though," he pointed out. The kitchen returned to normal. Emily brought his food to the table and poured tea for herself in the special blue mug she had drunk from since she was nine. As he ate, they talked of his own parents and his childhood in German-speaking Milwaukee. He liked that topic because he could remember it, and remembering made him feel safe. They lingered over his meal, each contented in the other's company.

Finally Emily rose from the table and began to clear away the dishes. "It's getting late," she said. "I'll look in on you tomorrow—maybe around six?"

"Fine."

"Okay then, sleep tight." She put on her coat and kissed him, and then she remembered his meds. "I almost forgot your pills. Stay put—I'll get them."

She went into his bedroom, switched on the lamp on the nightstand, and opened the drawer. As she slid her hand inside, she felt a hot rake of pain. She could smell the blood before she could see it, and she pulled the drawer wide before she carefully extracted her hand. Blood was everywhere, flowing freely from the four long gashes on the top of her hand, oozing and sticking around her palm, falling in great drops onto the wooden bottom of the drawer. Bending down, she could see the old-fashioned razor blades that had been stuck with some kind of caulk to the top of the frame. She straightened up, looking for something to stanch the bleeding, and saw Papa standing in the doorway.

"That's what happens to thieves," he shouted, the spittle flying from his mouth. "Thief! Robber! Get out of my house before I call the cops on you!"

THE REAL SELF

What must one do to hold someone in his identity when he has changed dramatically from the person one has always known and loved? Or when the person's self-conception is at radical odds with how other people see her? Or his identity is socially impossible, so that other people don't know what to do with him? Or the person isn't at all who she purports to be? What should we do to hold those whose identities lie at the limits of responsibility, where there is no settled, socially shared moral understanding of what we may or must do for them? In this chapter, I consider these and other hard cases of identity-work, bearing in mind the caution that hard cases make bad law, and that perhaps no good lessons for ethics can be drawn from them, either. I end with some further thoughts on second nature.

First, let's return to Emily, whom we left standing bleeding by Papa's open drawer. Her hand needs medical attention, but when she's seen to that, Papa needs *narrative* attention. A widely shared story has crept into her understanding of who he is that is injuring his identity, and she needs to replace it with a better one before the injury spreads any further. Like many other identity-damaging master narratives, the story has a surface plausibility that makes it appear innocent and harmless, and like all other identity-damaging master narratives, it's a morally degrading depiction of who the person is. It's the story of the real self—a story that's not only hurting Papa, but inflicting moral harm on Emily as well.

Recall that when Papa accuses Sonja of having stolen his car and demands to know what happened to the money, Emily's tale goes like this:

> At those moments the children got a glimpse of something hard inside him that was usually buried deep under many layers of kindness. A splinter of cruelty that his disintegrating self could no longer conceal.

Emily is picturing Papa with this splinter buried deep under many layers of paternal warmth and love—it's lodged in his core, where his heart should be. So then the layers of kindness, she seems to think, are just a civilized outer wrapping. Now that vascular dementia has rotted the wrapping so that long strips of it have begun to fall away, Emily can see who her father really is.

But does the term "real self" refer to anything actual? If, as I've argued, personal identities are narrative understandings of selves as they change over time, then a claim to know someone's real self presupposes something about either *what* the identity represents or *how* it represents it. I can think of three possibilities here. First, the claim might be less about the self than about the identity: a "real self" might be the one that a defective set of stories failed to capture. That the stories constituting an identity could misrepresent the person is certainly a possibility, but that doesn't seem to be what people mean when they say that they have finally discovered who someone really was—they seem to mean that they've discerned some core or inner self they hadn't seen before.

This suggests a second possibility, namely, that the reference is to a self that is credibly depicted by the narratives that constituted the person's identity *at a certain time*, which was then covered up by later accretions and is now uncovered again as a result of progressive dementia. But then we need to explain why that earlier point in time carries more narrative weight than any other, and how we can know that dementia has uncovered it. Is the thought here that dementia has loosened the inhibitions that formerly kept the authentic self in check? And are we privileging the self that's now uncovered because it's what is left at the end of the actions and choices the person has been responsible for in the course of his life? While it's true that some judgments about a person's life can only be made after one knows how various choices, deeds, or guesses ultimately turned out, there's no good reason to suppose that the knowledge of how things turned out must coincide precisely with the final years of the person's active biography. The consequences of some choices will be apparent much earlier; the ramifications of others may continue long after the person is dead. It's worth bearing in mind that the decline into dementia offers no more of a God's-eye view from which to judge a life than any other location; it, too, is a particular context with its own limited sight lines.

That leaves a third possibility, which is that the reference is to an aspect of the self depicted by a particular *storyline* that runs throughout a person's life, rather than attaching to a specific point in time. Does Emily suppose that the narrative binding together all the episodes of avarice in her father's life is the one that shows him as he really is? In that case, we need to explain why *that* story depicts something more real than the other stories that constitute the old man's identity. Was he often avaricious? Apparently not, or his children wouldn't remark on how seldom these episodes took place. Was he deeply cruel on the few occasions when avarice entered the picture at all? We have no reason to think so. In the absence of something that explains why we should give extra narrative weight to either an earlier point in the father's life or a particular storyline that runs throughout it, it's hard to see how one part of his self could be more real than all the others.

The philosopher and neurosurgeon Grant Gillett rejects the familiar conception of the self and mind whereby the higher brain keeps a tight rein on the hidden snakepit of wayward impulses that constitutes our real selves (Gillett 2002). This picture, which according to Gillett was promulgated in various guises by Freud, Darwin, and Jaspers, has been called into question by Wittgenstein, McDowell, and a number of others who have proposed instead that conscious thought is the product of socialization and training within a given form of life. "It is only as we engage in the everyday forms of life, those communal patterns of behavior where we learn to think and talk about things, that the contents of the mind take on a determinate shape," says Gillett (2002, 25). As we saw earlier, when we are very young children, we are initiated into the discursive activity that forms us as persons, and we live out our lives in this interaction between mind and world, continually shaping ourselves—and being shaped—through what we do, what others do to and with us, and the interpretations available to us in the social locations we inhabit.

Gillett likens the shaping of a human self to the weaving of a tapestry. And he insists that it would be as mistaken to say that the real self is the one degraded by dementia as to say that the real tapestry is the "mish-mash of disordered threads and fragments of intact weaving" that's left after the moths have gotten at it (Gillett 2002, 27). I believe Gillett is quite right about this, and that the narrative of the "real self" is pernicious. Emily has already wronged her father with that story, and if she were to actively endorse it (rather than tacitly presupposing it, which is all she's done with it at this point), she would, I submit, do her father lasting harm. Not only would she be misrecognizing him but also, because she'd be acting on the basis of that faulty story, she'd be treating him badly. And that in turn would derange her own identity: she'd see herself as an exploited and unloved daughter, merely a target of his abuse.

Moreover, she's damaging Papa's identity at a time when it's already heavily under siege. A series of tiny strokes have begun to disorder the *mental processes* that are most intimately bound up with her father's self at the same time as they have driven him to physical *expressions*—the razors in the drawer—that are appallingly off-kilter. Two of the four components of personhood are thus already malfunctioning. Increasingly, the disease will disable her father's capacity to contribute first-person stories to the narrative tissue by which he and others make sense of who he is; increasingly, the task of identity maintenance will fall on those who care for him. Because Emily employs a faulty identity-constituting story and to that extent fails to *recognize* who her father is, the third component of that maintenance has begun to misfire as well. Should she now *respond* to her father on the basis of that faulty story, all four components would misfire, and, in letting go of her father, she will have completed the destruction that the progressive dementia began.

Emily needs a counterstory—an identity-constituting story that resists the narrative of the real self and, in reidentifying Papa as a morally valuable person, mends the damage to her own identity as well (Nelson 2001). Repairing an identity requires *accuracy*: the story must be a faithful likeness. But faithful to what? To the man standing in the doorway in a towering rage as his daughter bleeds copiously into the drawer? No, for that isn't a story—it's just a snapshot of a particularly awful moment in this man's life. A story depicts that life over time, selecting characteristic episodes, interpreting the life through what it selects, and connecting itself to a vast web of other stories that also contribute to its overall meaning. A good story does all these things well.

Emily's counterstory needs to be such a story, more dynamic than Gillett's tapestry but just as sweeping. And if it includes episodes of anger or cruelty, it had better also include the many times Papa helped her with her homework, the soapbox racer he helped her build, the stories he read aloud to her, the voter canvassing they did together, the boxes of treats sent to her dorm room. For Emily's Papa is surely all of that, and it's all of that to which she must now respond.

She won't be able to stave off the ravages of the disease indefinitely. Dementia will continue to make inroads on Papa's memory, his language, his fine motor skills, his sense of his surroundings, his sense of himself. With her help, though, these losses can be held at bay for a little while, and when the man she has loved no longer exists, she'll remember him as he really was, not as the real self story depicted him.

REPUDIATED IDENTITIES

Emily's father is changing so fast that she has trouble holding him in his identity. But he doesn't repudiate that identity—it is slipping away from him whether he likes it or not. By repudiated identities, I mean identities that their former bearer has deliberately cast off, most typically, perhaps, because the person has undergone a radical conversion of some sort. Perhaps the person was raised in the Christian religion but now embraces Islam, possibly even taking a new name to underscore the change in her or his identity. Or perhaps the person has been an attorney in a large and faceless corporate law firm and now leaves all that behind to go live off the grid in Colorado. Or perhaps the person has finally managed to exit an abusive relationship and has vowed never to be that old submissive, meek, and cowering nonentity again. Whatever the radical shift, drastic alterations in someone's identity can leave others bewildered, struggling to understand her. Those nearest and dearest might be uncertain whether the person is authorized to perform the identity—the former partner of the abused spouse, for one, is most certainly not going to recognize her authority, nor might the Muslim convert's former coreligionists. Because the strength of a person's commitments can only be borne out over a period of time, no one (including the person himself) can judge, *from here*, at the moment of the conversion, whether the person truly has changed the course of his life. That can only be judged *from there*, much later, after the person has either stuck to it, fallen back into his old ways, or been driven off course by events outside his control (Williams 1981, 35).

For the new identity to count as genuine, the stories it comprises must be accurate portrayals of the person's actions and attitudes. The first-person stories that faithfully depict the attitude assure the bearer of the identity (and possibly the others) that she isn't just going through the motions; the second- and third-person stories that faithfully depict her actions assure others (and possibly the person herself) that the identity is properly hers. The backward-looking stories explain how she came to this life-changing moment, and the forward-looking stories plot the course she now intends to pursue. Unless that course is a morally impermissible one, it's probably best for others to hold her in her new identity, as that is a way of respecting her autonomy.

But all this raises the question of whether the person has genuinely *intended* to change course. To explain, I'll offer another story, this one from Sweden:

> A man, 75 years old, who was deeply involved in the vegetarian movement for many years, fell ill with Alzheimer's disease and was placed in a residential home, where in accordance with his previous habits he was served vegetarian meals. One day, by mistake, he happened to eat a portion of meatballs, potatoes, brown sauce, and lingonberries intended for another resident. He enjoyed it very much and at the next meal noticed for the first time that he was being served different food to all the others. The care workers persuaded him to eat his vegetarian meal, but the next day he refused point blank to eat "any special muck that's only for me."

His [case] worker discussed the situation with his wife who in no uncertain terms expressly forbade the staff to give him anything but vegetarian food. She insisted that it was against his (and her) convictions to eat meat, or "warmed-over dead body parts," as she put it. The staff tried to comply, but encountered vociferous protest at each meal from the man, who sometimes, with triumph and great delight, managed to appropriate food left over by someone else at the table.

The head of the unit and the staff were not sure how to handle this. Should they allow him to eat meat? What should they tell his wife? (Banks and Nøhr 2012).

In "Freedom of the Will and the Concept of a Person," Harry Frankfurt argues that the difference between a morally responsible person and a "wanton" is that persons don't just have desires—they have desires about their desires that can move them to act (Frankfurt calls such a desire a second-order volition). That is, they can evaluate the things they want, decide whether they *want* to want them, and act accordingly. "Wantons," by contrast, aren't capable of making—or just don't care to make—these evaluative judgments, so they simply act on whatever desires they happen to have (Frankfurt 1988a). As the man in this case suffers from a dementia that has progressed to the point where he can no longer be cared for at home, it seems highly probable that, in Frankfurt's terms, he is a wanton, no longer able to control his desire to eat meat by wanting not to have that desire. Because he isn't free to choose which desires to act on, it makes no more sense to hold him responsible for his actions than it does a drug addict, a toddler, or a chipmunk.

It doesn't take Frankfurt, though, to tell us that a man with well-advanced Alzheimer's disease is no longer morally responsible. The more interesting part of Frankfurt's analysis is that it helps us see why we shouldn't believe that the man has just changed his mind about eating meat. Changing one's mind, especially about something that involves a moral commitment, is not simply a matter of now choosing Y when you previously chose X. You also have to *repudiate* X (Nelson 2009). And that is a second-order desire, because repudiation is a matter of not wanting to want something anymore. If this desire moves you to act, you've exercised your second-order volition. After a person is demented enough to lose his second-order volition, however, he is no longer in a position to repudiate his commitments—to say to himself that, on reflection, he finds them less worthy than he previously did.

If that's right, then our reluctant vegetarian probably isn't capable of changing his mind. His previously formed evaluative judgment still deserves respect, though, because in making it and then sticking to it for so much of his life, the man defined himself morally: the story of his commitment to vegetarianism played some kind of role in his identity. We might not know exactly how much of a role, of course, because we don't know how centrally the commitment to vegetarianism figured into who he was. But his wife knows, and it may be her sense of his identity that now motivates her to insist that he not be given any meat. She might be making up for his inability to want what he wants by regulating his desires for him in accordance with her understanding of who he is.

But then the question arises whether he still is that person. One of the most devastating features of a progressive dementia is that it gradually disintegrates the person. That, as we've already seen in the case of Emily and her father, is all the more reason for those who have a long, shared history with the person to resist the damage as long as possible rather than cooperate with the disease's inexorable obliteration of the self. The wife may be trying to make sure that, as long as possible, her husband's actions conform with the identity to which he has, by his choices, contributed over all the years of his life.

It's certainly true that some of the stories that constituted his identity no longer have the same salience they once did, and new stories must be added to reflect the way the person changes over time. But the whole messy tissue of identity-constituting stories attaches to the person like a continually growing comet's tail, and it can't just be sheared off as the person's self disintegrates into dementia. Who the person has been is a part of who they are now—maybe even the most important part.

Still, we mustn't let the comet's tail wag the comet—or, at least, not altogether. So much has changed for this man that it may not seem reasonable to hold him to moral commitments that he no longer understands. There is so little left to him that it might seem cruel to deprive him of the few pleasures that yet remain. It might help if the husband could be fed in his room, where he wouldn't know what the others are eating, at least until he is too demented to care. If the staff can't manage that, though, and the man is made seriously unhappy by being denied meat, the wife may have to consider how important it is for him to remain true to the principles he has lived by. It may be very important indeed, but perhaps it mightn't matter as much as his present distress.

On the other hand, if his wife is a vegetarian on moral grounds, believing that it is wrong to eat animals because of the suffering this inflicts on sentient creatures (Singer 1975), she might be motivated less by the need to hold her husband in his identity than by the need to keep him from complicity in evildoing. Even then, of course, how he should be fed is not a decision she can make by herself, as the staff is involved as well, but because her life has presumably been closely intertwined with his for a very long time, her moral outlook merits special consideration. She, after all, is the only person in a position to consider what he would have done, had their roles been reversed and he been the one to decide what she should eat. Perhaps what matters most here is not the decision she makes, but how and why she makes it. And that way of thinking about it might, at the end of the day, be everybody's best option.

IMPOSSIBLE IDENTITIES

On October 3, 2002, at a party in Newark, California, seventeen-year-old Gwen Araujo was forced to expose her genitals in the bathroom of a private home. Her attacker yelled that "he was really a man," whereupon two young men who had had sex with her earlier that evening beat her severely, in full view of at least some of the other partygoers. They took the semiconscious girl out to the garage and choked her with a rope until they believed she was dead. Eventually, they wrapped her body, put it in the back of their truck, and dumped it in a remote wilderness area. Two weeks later, one of the suspects told the police what had happened and took them to the spot where the body lay (Reiterman, Garrison, and Hanley 2002, Calef 2002).

At the trial, the three men charged with first-degree murder and hate crimes used what has come to be known as the "trans panic defense"—the panic in question being the "extreme shock, amazement, and bewilderment" they experienced on learning of Araujo's "sexual deception." Their lawyers argued that the victim's "sexual fraud" and "betrayal" had understandably provoked their clients' violent response and insisted that the charge should be reduced to manslaughter. The jury failed to reach a verdict, and on retrial, two of the men received second-degree murder convictions, while the third pleaded *nolo contendere* to voluntary manslaughter. None of them was convicted of a hate crime (Bettcher 2007, 43–44).

A columnist for the *Iowa State Daily*, Zach Calef, claimed that the murder would not have occurred if Araujo had "been honest" with the men. Calef argued that their violence was understandable, as it was "simply a reaction to a form of rape." "Using lies and deception to trick them into having sex," he explained, is "as bad as rape." He acknowledged that, given the circumstances, murder was a bit much, but after all, "the men did what they did because Araujo violated them." "These men were truly violated," Calef repeated. "They were raped" (Calef 2002).

Calef's op-ed is a fine example of thinking that has been informed by the master narrative of the evil deceiver. According to that narrative, there are precisely two biological sexes, male and female, and these are firmly connected by nature to precisely two genders, masculine and feminine, that are the public expression of the private sexual reality. As a corollary, the genders are by nature heterosexual, and it's here that transphobia's link to homophobia becomes visible. If you have a penis, you are a man: God wills it so. And if you are a man and you present yourself as a sexually tempting woman, you are an evil deceiver, because not only are you taking on an unauthorized identity and therefore ruining the performance for the other actors, but also you are manipulating manly, heterosexual men into having sex with a man and thereby stripping them of their masculinity.

Fundamental to this master narrative is the distinction between appearance and reality: the gendered appearance must faithfully reflect the reality of the sex organs. "In this framework," argues Talia Mae Bettcher, "gender presentation (attire, in particular) constitutes a gendered appearance, whereas the sexed body constitutes the hidden, sexual reality. Expressions such as 'a man who dresses like a woman,' 'a man who lives as a woman,' and even 'a woman who is biologically male' all effectively inscribe this distinction" (Bettcher 2007, 48).

The master narrative creates a vicious double bind. If one is a transperson, one must either "disclose 'who one is' and come out as a pretender or masquerader, or refuse to disclose (be a deceiver) and run the risk of forced disclosure, the effect of which is exposure as a liar" (Bettcher 2007, 50). As those are the only two options there are, concludes Bettcher, "it would appear that this representational system actually prevents transpeople from existing at all" (55).

And that is what I mean by an impossible identity. When the identity-constituting stories circulating widely in your society allow you to be understood only as a liar or a deceiver, others are apt to treat you as if you have no right to exist. You are likely to be denied a job because your gender presentation doesn't match the M or F on your driver's license; you are subjected to beatings; you are raped "to teach you a lesson"; all too often, you are killed. There is no place for you anywhere, because there is no way for others to make sense of you. And what is worse, there's also no way for you to make sense of yourself. You may be firmly convinced that you are neither a liar nor a deceiver, but then you might also feel you are not a man, really, and not a woman, really, either. Those not-identities, though, don't offer any positive depiction of who you are. For that, you need counterstories that resist the evil deceiver narrative by offering concrete representations of the range of sexed and gendered possibilities—including the possibility of claiming for yourself one of the two genders with which most people identify.

White-skin privilege and middle-class status offer transpeople some protection from the evil deceiver narrative, to be sure, as does the growing social visibility of transpeople who hold public office, teach in schools and universities, or write about their experiences in blogs and newspaper columns. Still, counterstories to that narrative have been agonizingly slow on the uptake. The trans identity is likely to remain impossible until gender presentation ceases to represent genital status and becomes instead—as it is for any undamaged identity—an indication of how the transperson wants to be treated.

HYPOCRITES AND WANTONS

If the evil deceiver or other vicious master narratives purport to justify a powerful social group's abuse of a less powerful group by representing that group as not authorized to bear the identities it claims, there are also cases where people purport to bear an identity that truly isn't theirs. Some such people are con artists, others are hypocrites, and still others are wantons. As it's easy to understand the con artist, I want to focus here on the hypocrite and the wanton. In both cases, figuring out whether and how much of their identities to hold or let go of can be tricky.

The hypocrite abuses others' trust by acting as if she is committed to values that she doesn't in fact espouse. She plays a role that isn't hers, although she drops that role when she believes there's no audience. Then the others rely on her to act, and maybe act toward them, on the basis of the unauthorized identity. This is the preacher who thunders against marital infidelity in the pulpit while committing adultery in secret, or the owner of the daycare center who, when parents drop off their children and pick them up, makes a show of attending them lovingly but neglects them, or worse, when no parent is present.

The correct response to the hypocrite is to let go of her unauthorized identity in as public a manner as possible, but the trick is to recognize when she really isn't entitled to bear it. Two sorts of errors are possible here. The first is that the would-be unmasker might simply be wrong; the supposed hypocrite is in fact who she seems to be. The second is that the supposed hypocrite is not who the unmasker took her to be, but the unmasker incorrectly attributed an identity to her that she doesn't actually bear: think of the celebrity who is not nor ever claimed to be the "role model" his fans see him as. A failure to live up to someone else's mistaken view of one's identity is not a case of hypocrisy at all.

As should be patently clear by now, identity-work rests on a foundation of trust. We performers need to be able to rely on each other to play the roles we seem to be playing in the improvisations that constitute our interpersonal exchanges. If we couldn't trust the rest of the cast on the whole and for the most part, the shared cooperative activity that makes us persons would be impossible. The difficulty, of course, is that trust is also the atmosphere in which all kinds of unsavory practices flourish. In Annette Baier's words, "Exploitation and conspiracy, as much as justice and fellowship, thrive better in an atmosphere of trust" (Baier 1986, 231–32). Hypocrisy certainly thrives there. It's only because others trust the hypocrite to be who she seems to be that they accord her the moral and social credit she doesn't deserve.

The trust foundation can itself be defective if our trust is misplaced. This is not only what makes hypocrisy possible but also part of what went so badly wrong for Gwen Araujo: the men who had sex with her trusted that people with breasts who give blow jobs are "really" women, and their own identities as men took a beating when that story proved untrustworthy. Many oppressions require people to put their trust in stories—I've been calling them master narratives—that purport to justify and perpetuate abusive social systems.

Baier defines trust as reliance on another's good will: "When I trust another, I depend on her good will toward me" (Baier 1986,

235). And when I do this, of course, I necessarily lay myself open to the possibility that my trust is unmerited and the other might harm me. Her harming me when I trusted her not to, however, isn't enough to warrant my judgment that she's a hypocrite. Recall all the various ways that any of the four moments of identity-work can go wrong, even with the best will in the world. The harm could, in such cases, simply be the result of poorly executed or clumsy holding on her part, and then the proper response on my part is forgiveness. As Baier explains, "One thing that can destroy a trust relationship fairly quickly is the combination of a rigoristic unforgiving attitude on the part of the truster and a touchy sensitivity to any criticism on the part of the trusted. If a trust relationship is to continue, some tact and willingness to forgive on the part of the truster and some willingness on the part of the trusted both to be forgiven and to forgive unfair criticisms, seem essential" (238).

However, when the truster sees the trusted make many missteps in how she holds the truster in his identity, he would be foolish not to begin to wonder whether the trusted is actually trustworthy. If he suspects that the trusted is relying on concealment to keep the interchange going, he may well lose trust and start looking for evidence of whatever it is she seems to be hiding. Should he discover that she is relying on her skill at covering up or on his gullibility and ignorance, that very discovery will cure his gullibility and ignorance (Baier 1986, 255).

Possibly the most interesting aspect of the identity-work surrounding the hypocrite is not that of the unmasker's letting the hypocrite's false identity go, but rather the transformational possibilities in the identity of the unmasker himself. It takes a certain amount of courage to expose hypocrisy, as anyone who does it is at risk of being labeled a troublemaker, or meanspirited, or someone who rocks the boat. This reaction on the part of others is perhaps as it should be, given how essential trust is to the identity-work involved in personhood; where trust is the default setting, the evidentiary bar for exposing someone as false must necessarily be set fairly high. If, however, you've always been the kind of person who naively trusts everybody, is uncritically unreflective, or is overly concerned with what other people think of you, standing up to the hypocrite's deceit in a public unmasking says at least as much about who you are now as it says about the hypocrite. You are no longer going to unthinkingly believe what other people say, sacrifice your own integrity for an easy life, or allow others to prey upon your good nature. Here we see identity *construction* at work, as letting go of someone in this way changes who you yourself are.

The wanton, like the hypocrite, assumes identities he's not really entitled to, but unlike the hypocrite, his aim isn't to manipulate and deceive. He may be perfectly sincere in assuming a given persona, truly believing it is his. But because the values the persona expresses aren't ones he commits himself to, he continually changes to a new one, blowing wherever the wind takes him.

The wanton, recall, can't control his first-order desires by wanting some of them to move him all the way to action. "The essential characteristic of a wanton is that he does not care about his will," says Frankfurt. "His desires move him to do certain things, without its being true of him either that he wants to be moved by those desires or that he prefers to be moved by other desires. The class of wantons includes all nonhuman animals that have desires and all very young children. Perhaps it also includes some adult human beings as well" (1988a, 16–17). Frankfurt's example of such an adult is a drug addict who might both want to take the drug and want not to take it, but doesn't or can't care which of these conflicting desires becomes his will. "Since he has no identity apart from his first-order desires, it is true neither that he prefers one to the other nor that he prefers not to take sides" (18). He doesn't identify more heavily with one of them and withdraw himself from the other; he's mindlessly unreflective, incapable of—or uninterested in—evaluating his own wants and motives.

Suppose you are the parent of this wanton. Simon (we'll call him Simon) has been addicted to cocaine since he was sixteen years old, and you've lost track of all the times you've had to bail him out of jail, make good the sums of cash he stole from his grandparents, take him to the hospital, get him into treatment. You used to plead with him to think seriously whether this is how he wanted his life to go, but he just didn't seem to care. For ten years now, you've listened to him tell you sincerely that he's sorry he "made a mistake" and vow earnestly to go into rehab, only to tell you just as sincerely the next week that he can quit anytime he wants to, he's fine, he knows what he's doing so just leave him alone. And then a month later, he honestly believes that if you had just helped him a little, he wouldn't be in this mess. It's as if the bulk of the stories that constitute his identity are temporary, coming and going so fast that it's hard to see what they depict. When the narrative tissue representing a self is this unstable, it's impossible to hold the person in it—there's no fully established identity in which to hold him.

To be sure, there will be aspects of his identity that endure no matter what, and you may try to hold him in those: there is a sense in which he will always be your son, for example, and you might find you can't help but accord him the recognition and response that attach to that part of who he is. If Simon's wantonness causes the *social* relationship between you to break down, you can't repair it—let alone sustain it—all by yourself, any more than you can sustain a marriage if your spouse divorces you. Unlike marriage, though, the parent-child relationship is not one into which both parties entered freely, so there's no contract from which Simon can now withdraw.

Whether he likes it or not, the relationship between you is permanent; he can't altogether destroy the connection between you that says something important about who he is. Your shared history and the genetic tie between you arguably keep open the possibility of holding him, despite how little of him is left to hold.

IDENTITIES AT THE LIMITS OF RESPONSIBILITY

It might be objected that the bare biological tie between you and Simon has no moral significance at all, that the reason you can still hold him in even his attenuated form is that your lives have been intertwined for the last twenty-six years. So now I want to push on that bare biological tie, to see if it really contributes nothing to who somebody is. To do this, I'll have to first consider the special nature of the moral responsibilities involved in holding any close relative in his or her identity.

Most people tend to think that being closely related to others—being someone's sister or brother, mother or father, to take clear examples—gives us reasons to respond to their wants and needs in a special way: we're disposed to act for them out of love or for their sake. But philosophy hasn't been very helpful at justifying special responsibilities to family members. For instance, accounts of love, even familial love, often stress that feelings aren't under our control and so can't be seen as something for whose presence or absence we can be held responsible. Moral agency is therefore taken to be a matter of reasons, not feelings, and the sorts of reasons philosophers have offered for our responsibilities to others don't distinguish between strangers and close kin. They largely reduce to such concepts as "easy rescue" (the beneficiary has everything to gain; the helper, nothing to lose) or "compensatory justice" (I have wronged or harmed someone and now owe her something to mitigate the damage I caused, or have received benefits beyond my due and my acts ought to reflect that) and, most typically, voluntary and informed *consent* (I promised to help or willingly assumed a certain social role).

Those sorts of reasons, however, don't seem to explain in full the special responsibilities I have toward people I appropriately identify as family. Many of us share strong intuitions that I owe my children much more than easy rescue, and my duties to my parents are greater than would be explained by any damage I caused them. Nor does it seem that consent is doing very much of the work here: defeasibly, anyway, I owe my sister regard and support even though her being my sister has nothing to do with my having consented to anything.

Where there is a lengthy shared history between people—between Simon and his parents, for example—everything that they've gone through together can obscure how much moral pull is exerted by the sole fact of the familial connection. As Samuel Scheffler observes, "The more closely a person's reasons are seen as linked to his existing desires and motivations, the less scope there will be for distinguishing between the relationships that he has reason to value and the relationships that he actually does value. On the other hand, the less closely reasons are thought of as tied to existing desires, the more room there will be to draw such distinctions" (Scheffler 1997, 200).

So let's consider two people who are complete strangers to one another: half-brothers living on opposite sides of the country. Perhaps, when the mother of one boy became pregnant, her boyfriend broke up with her and moved far away, but later married and had another child. Perhaps the boys' mothers purchased sperm from the same vendor. Tell the story as you like it, but however they came into being, each grew up knowing nothing of the other's existence.

Now in his early forties, the one who lives in New York—we'll call him Ned—has just received a diagnosis of acute myeloid leukemia. He is about to face his first round of chemotherapy, and his doctor asks if he has any family members who might be interested in donating bone marrow. His seventy-year-old mother volunteers, but isn't histocompatible; he has no first cousins. It's then that Ned learns he has a half-brother. His mother, we will say, tells him the name of the sperm bank she used and from there he is able to trace Sam, one of the donor offspring, to his home in Santa Barbara.

The knowledge that he has a sibling changes how Ned understands himself; it's a small but significant addendum to who he takes himself to be. The stories that constitute his self-conception have long included the narrative of how he came into existence, so he's always assumed, as a logical possibility if nothing more, that he might have some sisters or brothers somewhere. But the identification of a specific person as an actual half-brother shifts something. There's a person out there in the world who maybe looks a little like him, shares the same bloodline, is a part of his family tree. That fact adds substance to the background against which he lives his life; it enriches his sense of belonging to *these* people, being part of *this* family. Here is someone he can ask for help in getting his cancer into remission. He picks up the phone.

Does the bare biological connection between Ned and Sam give Ned's request slightly more than commendatory force for Sam? Would Sam be doing something at least a little wrong if, by treating the request as if it had been made by a complete stranger, he failed to recognize Ned as his brother? That he and Ned are related is at the very least an *intelligible* reason, should Sam decide to get tested.

Suppose Sam wakes up the morning after Ned's call and says to his partner, Cassie, "I'm going to do it—I'll get tested."

Cassie, who knows how much Sam hates hospitals in general and dislikes being stuck by needles in particular, stares at him in disbelief. "Why on earth would you do that?"

"He's my brother," Sam replies.

Cassie could, of course, push back ("What do you mean, 'brother'? He's just some East Coaster who happens to share a couple of genes with you"), but it isn't as though Sam said something like "He called me on a Tuesday" or "I had the dream about the tuna again." Sam's reply is intelligible, it seems, in that it gestures toward something important about how Sam understands himself and the responsibilities he sees arising from that self-conception.

By the same token, Ned's response would be intelligible should he feel hurt if Sam dismissed his request as coming from a total stranger. Ned's reaction, of course, isn't determinative; he's a highly interested party, after all, and he would now have to look elsewhere for the bone marrow he needs. But added to this disappointment would be another that involves his identity: Sam wouldn't be recognizing that he and Ned are connected in a way that's importantly implicated in who they have each turned out to be.

That these responses would be intelligible, however, doesn't yet show that they're justifiable. To show that, we've got to find something in Ned's call on Sam that gives it prescriptive force.

On some analyses—Robert Goodin's (1997), Margaret Urban Walker's (1998), Marian Verkerk's (2012)—vulnerability is a key consideration in understanding special responsibility: roughly, we have special responsibilities to those whose interests are vulnerable to our actions and choices. So we might consider the argument that Ned is especially vulnerable to Sam's response to him. Not all vulnerabilities are equally salient, though. If I were particularly hurt by your failure to lend me money because, say, we both happen to be able to wiggle our ears and that biological fact strikes me as crucial, my idiosyncratic vulnerability would not be your problem.

Is the bare biological tie between Ned and Sam just as irrelevant from a moral point of view as a shared ability to wiggle one's ears? We can imagine someone who thinks so kindly explaining Ned's mistake: he has failed to distinguish between the genetic and social senses of *brother*. The social sense does, according to this person, give rise to justifiable normative expectations, but genes are just genes, and no prerogatives or responsibilities attach to them. Ned has merely committed the error of transferring the moral penumbra surrounding the social sense of *brother* to the genetic sense, where it doesn't belong.

That explanation seems unsatisfactory. The connection between Ned and Sam isn't "simply biological," if that phrase suggests facts unmoored from human practices and feelings. Common attitudes and actions strongly testify to the depth of importance people assign to the biological dimension of family making: consider Ned's and Sam's own mothers' desire to have children of their bodies. Indeed, most human societies have organized the nurture, protection, and socialization of offspring around that "simply biological" connection. We might perhaps be able to imagine other arrangements—say, the one that Plato had in mind for the Guardians of the Republic, where children are reared in common, with no special attachments to or claims on any particular elders, and no distinction made between genetic siblings and others of their cohort. I'm suspicious of this, though. Had Plato himself ever been pregnant, he might not so easily have dismissed the intensity and duration of the physical intimacy between the gestating woman and the fetus she was calling into personhood. That's a tie that can be broken, of course, but there seems no good reason to break it routinely as an established social practice, as doing so is bound to violate the feelings of love and protection most parents have for their offspring. As well, some other way would have to be found to give children the identities that connect them to the past as well as singling them out specially from all others of their own generation.

In any case, that's not how we do it. The general social practice in families is to assign responsibilities and make people accountable to one another on the basis of genetic ties *as well as* the ties by which people bind themselves voluntarily. To be sure, Ned's identity as Sam's half-brother may not be the only morally salient consideration here. Many kind-hearted strangers might be willing to respond positively to Ned's request purely on the principle of easy rescue, or because they have voluntarily put their name on a donor registry. But the biological tie between the two men is, I think, a reason that makes its own contribution to the moral shape of the situation.[1]

FURTHER THOUGHTS ON SECOND NATURE

An insistent sound somewhere. She swam up out of a deep warm sleep and fumbled on the nightstand for the phone. What time was it, anyway? The phone display read a little after three in the morning.

"Hello?"

"Ms. Mencken?" The voice was unfamiliar.

"Yes? Who's calling?"

"I'm Meredith Whitehall, the night supervisor at The Pines—"

Oh dear god. It was Mom.

---

1. This discussion owes a great deal to James Lindemann Nelson, my coauthor for published work on the ethics of families.

"—and I'm afraid your mother isn't well. She's very agitated and asking for you, and we think it might help if you—"

"I'll be right there."

Kate pulled on jeans and a sweatshirt, pushed her feet into a pair of shoes, and found the car keys. This was the third time in two months that she'd received such a call, though never so late at night. She didn't mind going, really she didn't; she'd asked the staff to please let her know any time Mom needed her. As she drove down the dark highway, the guilty despair that had dogged her constantly since she'd moved her mother into the nursing home was lifted for a moment by a flicker of hope. What if Mom had asked for her by name? The elderly woman didn't have many words left anymore. Please let her call me Kate just one last time.

She could hear the wailing all the way down the corridor. Running to her mother's room, she flung the door open to see all the lights on, her mother wild-eyed in a corner, two aides trying to calm her, and her roommate sitting bolt upright in bed, sobbing.

Kate ran to her mom. "What's all this noise, Sweetheart?"

It was a bad move. Panicked, her mother swung a punch, hitting Kate squarely in the mouth. The wailing ascended into a shriek, and then it was kicks and more punches and blood everywhere until the aides managed to restrain the frightened woman. But they couldn't restrain her tongue. She screamed abuse at Kate, using filthy epithets Kate didn't even know she knew, her face contorted with hate as she tried to lunge at her daughter again. Kate backed out of the room, the iron taste of blood hot in her mouth. Weeping silently, she cupped one hand under her chin and carefully spat out a tooth.

This elderly woman is not, of course, morally responsible for the vicious attack on her daughter—the amyloid plaques building up in her brain have not only erased most of her words; they have destroyed her moral agency. Once she was a loving mother, kind, gentle, proud of her dear Kate. Now Alzheimer's disease has consumed most of those ways of being.

In any progressive dementia, a point is reached when speech begins to misfire, becoming clumsy, then garbled, and finally vanishing altogether. Kate's mother loses her conceptual grip, forgetting what a spoon is for, or what goes in a refrigerator. She loses her sense of what is ridiculous, what is kind, cruel, or courageous, and when an utterance is an assertion, an appeal, an explanation. She can no longer read other people's bodily expressions of their feelings, desires, or intentions, and her inability to make sense of them means she can't respond to them properly, either. The disease has almost destroyed her second nature and, with it, her self.

Once Kate's mother is stripped of the capacity to participate in personhood that has been second nature to her, it would seem that she will be condemned to the status of a nonperson. This, we might conclude, is the tragedy of Alzheimer's. The disease takes away everything that matters about being human.

I argue that this conclusion is false. We can see it's false if we reflect on the process whereby she gained her second nature in the first place. Recall that it has taken a great many people—indeed, the customs and institutions of an entire society—to give Jack-Jack, Ellie, Kate's mother, and everyone else the language, the shared interest and feeling, the modes of response, the sense of right and wrong, and all the rest of it that constitute our second nature. And it was in the course of our initiation into second nature that a great many people taught us how to participate in the practice of personhood.

But when she was so young that she could not yet take part in the practice herself, Kate's mother—like Carla—was *held* in personhood by the people who cared for her. Then, her ability to express frustration, pleasure, or other mental states gave her parents and other caregivers something on which to anchor their recognition and response—they engaged in a one-sided practice of personhood. Now that she once again lacks the capacity for active participation in the practice, she may still retain enough mental functioning to be held in personhood by the other persons who touch her life.

This holding is a kind of preservative love. Sara Ruddick reserved that term for the maternal work of keeping children safe from *physical* harm (Ruddick 1989, 65–70). I extend it, here, to encompass safekeeping from *moral* harm—the harm of being cast out of the special social and moral status accorded to persons. To fail to hold people with progressive dementia in personhood—to treat them as nonpersons, as nothing more than a body to be washed, clothed, and fed, for example—is to cut them off from the social relationships that continue to contribute to their humanity. And to do it to someone who can still be held in personhood would be the real tragedy of Alzheimer's.

It can be objected that for people with advanced dementia who no longer have a second nature, not being held in personhood is no tragedy. To explain how this could be, let's consider a different sort of case, in which the refusal to hold in personhood someone who lacks a second nature clearly *is* a tragedy.

In Werner Herzog's 1974 film, *Jeder für sich und Gott gegen alle* (in English *The Enigma of Kaspar Hauser*), which is closely based on events that actually took place in the early years of the nineteenth century, the baby Kaspar is snatched from his cradle and forced to live for the next seventeen years imprisoned in a dark cell, with no human companionship of any kind. The only person he ever sees is a man in a black overcoat and top hat, who gives him bread and water. In 1828 (although Kaspar, of course, has no idea what year it is, or even what a year is), the man pulls Kaspar out of his cell; teaches him to write his name, walk, and say a few phrases; and abandons him on a street in Nuremberg. The object of much curiosity, he becomes an exhibit in a circus before the kindly Herr Daumer rescues him, teaches him to read and write, and exposes him to music. Kaspar learns quickly, but he is always very strange, unfit to live on his own and requiring constant care.

Kaspar never acquired a second nature and so never fully became a person. All he has is his animal nature, like that of any other beast in the wild. And as Alison Gopnik observes, "A wild animal or a wildflower is fully an animal or a flower. But a wild child, like the famous Wild Child of Aveyron, is a damaged and injured child" (Gopnik 2009, 67). The tragedy here, of course, is that he need not have been damaged. Had he not been left utterly alone all those years, he could have lived as persons do, caring for and about others, participating in civic life, practicing a trade or a profession, enjoying his evenings in a tavern, perhaps marrying and having children. In short, he could have had a *human* life. That he didn't, because he was torn from those who would have held him in personhood until he was old enough to be a person on his own, was a terrible wrong.

By contrast to people like Kaspar Hauser, however, people in the more advanced stages of a progressive dementia can never again have the experiences of personhood. Their minds have been damaged not by human agency but by the ravages of the disease, and to date there is no known repair. And so, our objector goes on to argue, as the goods of personhood are closed to them no matter what we do, it's no tragedy for them to be treated like any other damaged animal. In any case, the objector adds, they won't know the difference. For both those reasons, they haven't been wronged.

Let's start with the second reason: they won't know the difference. The assumption here is that what you don't know can't hurt you, but that strikes me as dubious. There are certainly cases in which it might be true—for example, your grown son narrowly avoided a head-on car crash the other day and didn't see any point in alarming you—but in other cases you can be wronged even if you never find out. Consider the rich aunt who died and left you half her estate, but due to the machinations of your evil cousin, who was also her lawyer, the will was suppressed and all the money went to him. You had no expectations in the matter and are delighted by his good fortune, but it seems clear that he wronged you, even though you will never know it.

The trouble with the rich aunt example, though, is that while it shows that there is such a thing as an unexperienced wrong, it doesn't fit the present case. The wrong done to you in stealing your inheritance is that your interests are set back, whereas people in advanced stages of dementia don't have comparable interests. So consider a closer example: a good friend and colleague is jealous of your recent professional success. Rather than discuss it with you, she behaves toward you as she always has, but behind your back she speaks contemptuously of your work to other colleagues. They aren't influenced by her slander and don't want to hurt your feelings, so they never tell you, but it seems to me that even if you never learn of her treachery, she has wronged you all the same. Here the wrong is not that your interests have been set back—your false friend hasn't hurt your career. The harm is, rather, a respect harm. She has maliciously let go of your identity, treating you with unwarranted contempt.

At this point, the objector might reply that the wrong done in both these cases is to deprive you of any recourse. If you knew about what had been done to you, you could take certain steps: sue to regain your inheritance, for example, or break off relations with your perfidious friend. People in the late stages of dementia, by contrast, can't know or care how they are treated, so they haven't been similarly wronged. But this argument won't do. It puts the cart before the horse, because the reason you need recourse in the first place is that you *have* been wronged. To be sure, depriving you of recourse compounds the initial wrong, but that exists regardless of whether you are in a position to redress it.

That people like Kate's mother can't know or care whether they are held in personhood is a recapitulation of the first reason for denying that there is a tragedy here, namely, that the goods of personhood are closed to them. To this I want to reply that even if they are, it matters to us now how we will be treated later. Who I am *then* isn't just an old woman lashing out violently in a nursing home, for I am always, until I die, the being who has lived the whole of my life. To have lived it as a person is to have taken my proper place in the social world that lets us make selves of each other. If, at the end of my life, I can no longer actively participate in the complicated practice of self making, I would hope to be treated with the respect that is due to any citizen of that world, by being held inside it.

Chapter 6

What and When to Let Go

Identities at the End of Life

We need, in love, to practice only this: letting each other go.
For holding on comes easily; we do not need to learn it.

—Rainer Maria Rilke

It was Tosca's apartment, really. The living room was uncarpeted for greater ease of sliding and chasing, should she care to bat her catnip mice under the sofa. Two large cardboard boxes also lay on the hardwood floor, should she care to lurk inside. A pole with perches set at different heights stood before the picture window, should she care to survey the passing scene. And while two scratching posts were available for her use, the state of the furniture clearly proclaimed that she preferred to sharpen her claws on the upholstery. The only concession to her besotted keeper's own taste and convenience was an elaborate sound system flanked by rows of vinyl recordings of Baroque and nineteenth-century music, heavy on the Italian composers.

Charlie looked in on Edmund and Tosca about once a week, sometimes bringing a new CD, sometimes just bringing faculty gossip. It had been twenty years since the elderly professor retired, but he liked to keep abreast of departmental politics, even though he'd outlived all the faculty of his generation, and besides, he enjoyed having Charlie to talk to. The gray tabby would jump onto Charlie's lap and demand to be petted, with special attention to the white bib under her chin, and Edmund would tell him all about how clever Tosca was, which operas she liked best, and what the vet had said at her last check-up. He'd tell him about his former students, too, some of whom had kept in touch, and he'd quiz him about his latest research, since, like Edmund, Charlie was a specialist in medieval European history.

When Edmund called Charlie that evening, frightened, to tell him he couldn't breathe for the pressure on his chest, Charlie broke the speed limit getting him to the hospital and stayed with him while they diagnosed a heart attack in progress. The cardiologist on call told them Edmund needed a cardiac catheterization so that she could see exactly which arteries or vessels were blocked. After they prepped Edmund, Charlie did his best to reassure him. "I'll be right here," he promised. "You're going to be okay."

"Who'll look after Tosca?"

"It's all taken care of. I phoned your neighbor."

"If I'm dying, don't let me die here. Let me die at home, with Tosca."

"You're not dying."

"Do they know that you're my decision maker if anything goes wrong?" he asked.

"Yeah, it's in your chart. Nothing's going to go wrong, though. They're going to fix you up."

"I want to die at home."

"I know."

In the middle of the catheterization, Edmund sustained a second, massive heart attack. He underwent an emergency double-bypass surgery, and when it was over, they took him to the cardiac intensive care unit. They let Charlie see him the next morning, an ashen-faced eighty-five-year-old man on a heart monitor with an IV drip and God knew how many tubes running from his body to wherever it was that they were supposed to go.

Over the next two weeks, Charlie couldn't see much improvement, though the cardiologist, Dr. Stoddard, remained consistently upbeat. At first, Edmund recognized Charlie but wasn't strong enough to talk much, so Charlie downloaded quantities of Edmund's favorite music—Mozart, Verdi, Boccherini, Puccini—onto his iPod, and Edmund listened to it for hours at a time. His heart was so badly damaged that it couldn't pump adequately, which put stress on his kidneys to the point where they, too, began to fail. He was too sick to eat, so they fed him with a nasogastric tube. Then, in his third week in the intensive care unit, just as his kidneys were starting to respond to treatment, he developed pneumonia. When Charlie came to see him the next day, there was a breathing tube down his throat, and he was on a ventilator.

"What happened?" he asked his nurse.

"He had trouble breathing."

"But you know he doesn't want this—"

"It's only temporary, just for seventy-two hours, to give the antibiotics a chance to clear up the pneumonia."

Charlie didn't like where things were headed but agreed that the tube could stay in, on the strict understanding that this was to be only temporary. He'd already gone over with Dr. Stoddard the standardized form Edmund had signed five years ago, titled "Declaration of a Desire for a Natural Death," which stipulated that "if my condition is determined to be terminal and incurable, my physician may withhold or discontinue extraordinary means, artificial nutrition or hydration, or both." It looked like Edmund was sliding further into just the kind of medical morass he didn't want, and Charlie would have to get him out of it.

They kept Edmund sedated so he wouldn't fight the ventilator. When the seventy-two hours were up, they gave him a lung function test, which, in the hospital's unlovely parlance, he failed. Time to call a halt, Charlie thought. Not only has this gone far enough, it's gone too far. He made an appointment with Dr. Stoddard for later that afternoon and asked him to take Edmund off the ventilator so he could die in peace.

"Take him off the ventilator?" Stoddard said. "Why, you mustn't even think of it. Professor Randolph isn't dying, you know. His kidneys are doing much better. *Much* better. In fact, his urine output is back up to normal. And the pneumonia is clearing up, too. No, no, we need to be thinking more positively. For one thing, we need to get his weight up. The nasogastric tube seems to be bothering him, so I'd like to implant a PEG tube into his abdomen—just a simple surgical procedure—and I also think his breathing tube would be more comfortable for him if we performed a tracheotomy."

Charlie was appalled. "But you can't!" he protested. "He's been very clear from the beginning that he doesn't want to end up like this. Please don't keep doing things to him. Please—it's got to stop."

Stoddard tapped his fountain pen on the desk. "I sympathize with what you're going through, but you have to understand that patients don't always mean what they say. I've seen it so often, people telling me they don't want to live if it means being on oxygen the rest of their lives, or being bed-bound, or having to go into a nursing home. But then when they find themselves in that situation, they discover it's not as bad as they thought it would be." He gave him a wry little smile. "It's certainly better than being dead."

"How do you know *Edmund* didn't mean what he said? You can't just bulldoze right over his express wishes!"

"But he might have changed his mind. There's still a chance that he'll pull through. Maybe not to where he can go home, but to where he can still get some pleasure out of his life. I can't in good conscience—"

"But he doesn't want—" They spoke simultaneously.

Stoddard compressed his lips, as if to keep the wrong words from escaping. Then he pushed back his chair and stood up. "There's a perfectly simple way to settle this," he said. "Professor Randolph is only temporarily incapacitated, you know. Let's just take him off sedation, and when he wakes up, we can ask him whether he wants us to continue treatment."

Charlie stood, too. "No. No, don't do that. I know what he wants. I know *him*. He wants his cat. He wants his music. He wants his old life back. And if he can't have those things, he wants to die quietly. At home, if possible. But if not, at least without all the tubes."

He argued it out with Stoddard for another half-hour, but he might as well have saved his breath. The cardiologist remained adamant: it wasn't time to give up on Edmund. So there they were. Charlie didn't have any idea what to do next. His biggest fear was that when they waked Edmund the next morning, he would say yes and improve just enough to end up in a nursing home, with one complication after another until he finally died. I've got to stop that, he thought, but I can't see how. It's not right. None of this is right. Somehow, I've got to convince them to let him die tonight, before he has a chance to get better.

If, as Rilke observed, we need in love to practice letting each other go, it seems we must sometimes also practice holding on. What can Charlie be thinking when he tries to deprive Edmund of the chance to decide his own care for himself? How can those who love the dangerously ill best hold them in their identities, and when is it time to let go? In this chapter, we'll consider disagreements such as the one between Charlie and Dr. Stoddard, but also the disagreements that arise among family members, each trying to hold the dying person in their own way. We'll then take a look at how the dying hold the living in their identities and what the living can do to make that kind of holding misfire. And finally we'll consider the identity-work that goes on after someone has died: both how the dead hold the living in various ways and the acts of preservative love by which the living hold the dead.

We'll start with Charlie's dilemma. Many people's preliminary intuitions will doubtless line up on the cardiologist's side of the disagreement: if the patient can speak for himself, he should speak for himself, and Charlie shouldn't try to foreclose the possibility that he might make a decision Charlie doesn't like. Charlie, while surely well intentioned, exceeds his authority by insisting that Edmund not be given the opportunity to change his mind. It's Edmund's life, when all is said and done, and if he now finds he can settle for a severely diminished version of it, it's not Charlie's place to stop him. These are widely shared moral understandings, justifiable on the grounds of respect for patient autonomy and the value of human life. I have no wish to unseat them; they're increasingly necessary in an age when professional health care givers wield such tremendous power over their patients. I want to complicate those understandings, though, by suggesting that Charlie might, under conditions of extreme duress, be doing his best to hold Edmund in his identity.

BACKGROUND

Before I begin, a little stage setting is in order. In wealthy nations where health care delivery is driven by continuous advances in biomedical technology, it's not uncommon for people to fear what

Philippe Ariès called a "wild" death. In *The Troubled Dream of Life,* Daniel Callahan explains that by a wild death Ariès meant the death of technological medicine, "marked by undue fear and uncertainty, by the presence of medical powers not quite within our mastery, by a course of decline that may leave us isolated and degraded." A tame death, by contrast, is "tolerable and familiar, affirmative of the bonds of community and social solidarity, expected with certainty and accepted without crippling fear" (Callahan 1993, 26). Callahan notes that in societies where wild deaths predominate, doctors are pushed by an imperative to take life-sustaining technology all the way up to the point where it becomes harmful and only then to withdraw or withhold it. But because of medicine's continuing failure to achieve the precision necessary for this kind of brinkmanship, he argues, more and more people experience the violence of "death by technological attenuation" (Callahan 1993, 41).

Callahan somewhat injudiciously writes as if a death accompanied by technology were by definition violent, but that's surely wrong. Many people welcome whatever technological assistance they can get at the end of life and are not at all degraded by it. Where such a death is *violent* is when the technology is used to *violate* the person, contemptuously disregarding the person's bodily integrity, injuring or shattering the person's sense of self. In this respect, technology becomes violent in the same way that sexual intercourse becomes violent: when it is no longer welcome.

According to Callahan, the wildness of death has also prompted a shift in what counts as dying: patients in the United States are often not defined as dying until their doctors judge that no further technological interventions will improve their condition. If he's right, it's no wonder that Dr. Stoddard isn't ready to stop treating Edmund—or, for that matter, that he's not yet willing to acknowledge the authority of Edmund's advance directive. The medical practice that surrounds the culture of wild death is governed by a particularly powerful norm: it's worse to err on the side of letting a patient die prematurely than to err by overtreating the patient.

One reason that the norm in favor of treating is particularly powerful is that, as Robert Veatch has argued many times, physicians have a role-related bias in favor of treatment:

> Members of special social and professional groups hold special, atypical values. This is true of all professionals, not just physicians. Something led them to choose their profession; they believe in its goals and believe it can do good things. They should favor the use of society's resources for their profession. This is not necessarily because they will earn more if more of society's resources are devoted to their sphere; it is more because they have an unusual view about the value of the services in the field to which they have given their lives.
>
> Imagine if professors of philosophy were asked to decide the number of required courses in philosophy in a college curriculum. They would plausibly make the wrong choice, not only because they would have an economic interest in remaining employed, but importantly, because they have an unusual view about the value of studying philosophy. Likewise, clinicians should be expected to make value tradeoffs atypically. (Veatch 1997, 396; see also Veatch 1973)

If Veatch is right and their unusual view about the value of treatment causes most physicians to believe that technological support and treatment should be given until they no longer work, then, from their point of view, the burden of proof is on the patient to show that refusing further life-sustaining treatment is reasonable. Ideally, the principle of respect for patient autonomy swings the burden back in the opposite direction, but there's a catch: in the physician's epistemic environment, refusal of treatment can be seen as a sign that the patient is not mentally competent and therefore not capable of exercising her autonomy. So, often, the bias in favor of treatment remains in place.

HOLDING EDMUND

It's against this background that I want to consider what Charlie might be doing as he urges that Edmund be allowed to die before he wakes. His reasons might have nothing to do with how he holds Edmund in his identity, so let me start by enumerating those more familiar considerations, just to get them out of the way. First, he could be thinking that if Edmund were awakened and asked if he wanted treatment to continue, he might assent out of fear of dying, rather than because he has given the matter careful thought. In that case, Edmund's assent would not be one he had reflectively endorsed and so wouldn't be truly his own; it would be fear, not an act of Edmund's own autonomy, that would move him to action. Second, Charlie might be worried that because Edmund is in such unfamiliar surroundings, he might be particularly susceptible to decisional pressures: there is a body of research, beginning with the infamous Milgram experiments, offering powerful evidence that people are highly suggestible to figures in authority, even when told to do things they ordinarily wouldn't do. As John Doris has concluded, "The experimental record suggests that situational factors are often better predictors of behavior than personal factors, and this impression is reinforced by careful examination of behavior outside the confines of the laboratory" (Doris 2002, 2). If Charlie were bearing this research in mind, he could be afraid that because the authority figures in Edmund's environment—in white coats and carrying stethoscopes—are biased in favor of treatment, Edmund will assent to treatment against his own better judgment, and again he wouldn't be acting autonomously. Third, Charlie might think that the mere ability to understand what he is asked and to say yes in reply is no indication that he's competent to determine his course of care. Given the bludgeoning that Edmund's body has sustained in the last three weeks, including two heart attacks, one cardiac catheterization, one double-bypass surgery, kidney failure, pneumonia, and lung failure, Charlie might be doubting Edmund's ability to think clearly, even if it turned out that he could respond when spoken to. In that case, his assent would once more be heteronomous, as it would be his illness making the decision rather than Edmund himself.

It may well be that Charlie is motivated by some combination of these considerations. In addition, though, he might be doing something more interesting—namely, trying to hold Edmund in his identity. Under ordinary conditions, of course, mentally and morally competent adults can do the lion's share of maintaining their own identities. Before his heart attacks, it was out of Edmund's sense of himself as an eighty-five-year-old retired college professor, opera buff, and cat owner that he went about his daily business. Even then, of course, he wasn't doing the work of identity maintenance all by himself. The familiarity of his surroundings and his day-to-day relationships also helped him maintain his self-conception. His cat Tosca, simply by jumping into his lap and purring, or demanding that he feed her, reminded him who he was. Sleeping in his own bed, listening to recordings from his own music library, and cooking his supper on his own stove also contributed to his self-conception. His neighbor, acting on the basis of narratives she contributed to his identity, greeted him with a friendly "How's Tosca?" The clerk at the record store, acting out of his own sense of who Edmund was, saved the new Riccardo Muti recording of the *Verdi Requiem* for him. By listening sympathetically to his stories, Charlie also affirmed Edmund's sense of himself as himself.

Serious injury or illness, rape, assault, the death or divorce of a spouse, and other traumas can and frequently do play havoc with one's identity. To be critically ill for more than a few days is to lose control over your physical and mental processes. It puts a stop to your professional and social activities and interferes with your memories, hopes, plans for the future, and ongoing projects. It usually involves hospitalization, which means that you are uprooted from your familiar surroundings; denied access to cherished people, pets, and objects; and thrust into a milieu governed by insider understandings to which you aren't privy. All of this contributes to a disintegration of your self. The physician Eric Cassell conceptualizes the sense of this disintegration as *suffering*: to suffer is to feel yourself coming undone. Suffering persists, writes Cassell, until the threat to the identity has passed or until the integrity of the identity can be reestablished in some manner (Cassell 1982).

It's when we suffer in Cassell's sense of the word that we most need the help of others to hold us in our identities. Torn out of the contexts and conditions in which we can maintain our own self-conceptions, we run the risk of losing sight of who we are—at least temporarily—unless someone else can lend a hand. Charlie, whether or not he conceived of it in this way and whatever else he might also be doing, could well have been trying to maintain Edmund's identity for him.

The Edmund he knows is Tosca's owner, the elderly opera lover who lived contented in his oddly furnished little apartment and claimed him as his friend. The stories by which he constitutes Edmund's identity are woven around his interactions with him, and they include the stories Edmund has told him about his life and times. Dr. Stoddard, on the other hand, doesn't know Edmund as well as Charlie does, so the stories that constitute his understanding of Edmund are much more likely to be drawn from the cache of widely circulating, medically shared master narratives that doctors use to depict patients as a group. He's never seen this particular patient before this illness, and since his hospitalization, Edmund's been so ill that the doctor hasn't had much of a chance to get to know him.

So while Charlie is caring for someone we might call Tosca-Edmund, the doctor sees mainly Patient-Edmund: the Edmund that Tosca-Edmund has become as a result of serious illness. These aren't really two distinct people, of course. There is bodily continuity, his memories and personal history haven't altered, and his Social Security number remains the same. If what we wanted to know was "Is he the person who was admitted to the hospital three weeks ago?"—Schechtman's reidentification question—the answer is yes. But if what we want to know is "Does the tissue of stories that used to constitute his identity still represent him accurately?"—the characterization question—the answer may be no (Schechtman 1996).

On an identity view of the moral situation, then, the quarrel between doctor and proxy might easily never have been about respect for Edmund's autonomy—they both might well agree that, if he's still autonomous, Edmund should determine for himself the kind of treatment he will receive. What they, on my hypothesis, disagree about is *which* self should do the determining. The proxy thinks it should be Tosca-Edmund, who exercised his autonomy by drawing up an advance directive. The doctor thinks it should be Patient-Edmund, who, if competent, might override Tosca-Edmund's wishes.

Although we've moved the locus of the disagreement, the correct strategy for resolving it might still be the one Dr. Stoddard originally proposed: if you want to know which self should determine Edmund's future, why not wake him up and ask him? The difficulty with moving the old strategy to the new locus, though, is that the outcome is rigged: the current self will naturally choose in its own favor, so when you ask the question you already have a pretty good idea of what the answer will be. If there is a Patient-Edmund distinct from Tosca-Edmund and he is mentally capacitated when he wakes, he will say that he and not Tosca-Edmund is now in charge.

But, it might be objected, the outcome is always rigged. It was just as rigged when Tosca-Edmund signed the advance directive. What he was doing when he signed it was trying to ensure that the Dr. Stoddards of this world would never get the upper hand, and presumably he wouldn't have wanted some later Patient-Edmund to override him either. Why, now that so much has changed, isn't it Patient-Edmund's turn to call the shots?

To get help with this question, we might look to Ronald Dworkin, who, in *Life's Dominion: An Argument about Abortion, Euthanasia, and Individual Freedom*, suggests that if we want to understand why we care about how we die, we must first understand why we care about how we live. He distinguishes between two kinds of interests that give our lives their value and meaning. *Experiential* interests are those that have to do with pleasures or satisfactions. He describes them this way:

> We all do things because we like the experience of doing them;
> playing softball, perhaps, or cooking and eating well, or watching
> football, or seeing *Casablanca* for the twelfth time, or walking in
> the woods in October, or listening to *The Marriage of Figaro*, or
> sailing fast just off the wind, or just working hard at something.

Pleasures like these are essential to a good life—a life with nothing that is marvelous only because of how it feels would be not pure but preposterous. (Dworkin 1993, 201)

Critical interests, on the other hand, are those that give life its deeper and more lasting meaning and lend it coherence. We establish close friendships, build a career, raise children, pursue artistic or political goals not only because we want the pleasurable experiences these things offer but because we believe our lives as a whole will be the better for taking up these projects. "Even people whose lives feel unplanned," says Dworkin, "are nevertheless often guided by a sense of the general style of life they think appropriate, of what choices strike them as not only good at the moment but in character for them" (Dworkin 1993, 202). It's this tendency to want to stay in character, as it were, that helps to explain why many of us care not only about how our lives go on but about how our lives end. As we approach death, it's not just that we want to avoid pain for ourselves and unpleasant burdens for our families; we also want to avoid dying in ways that aren't consistent with how we have lived. As Dworkin puts it, most people "want their deaths, if possible, to express and in that way vividly to confirm the values they believe most important to their lives" (Dworkin 1993, 211).

Because Dworkin assigns greater moral significance to an individual's critical interests than to her experiential interests, he endorses what he calls the *integrity* view of autonomy—the view that people should be free to act even in ways that clearly conflict with their current best interests, if that's what they see as preserving their sense of who they are. And this, he thinks, holds for exercises of "precedent autonomy" as well. Which is to say that Edmund's interest in living his life in character would have included an interest in determining what would happen to him later, under conditions of serious illness that he had never encountered, even if he misjudges what that experience will be like. His advance directive, stipulating that he wants a "natural" death and appointing as proxy decision maker a friend who knows him, is a mechanism for seeing to it that his critical interests, and not just his experiential ones, will be honored. Dworkin, then, has a lot to say in support of Tosca-Edmund's claims to be in charge.

Rebecca Dresser, on the other hand, has argued that experiential interests must take precedence when patients are too ill to say what they want. For one thing, people don't seem to value exercises of precedent autonomy. "Surveys show," she writes, "that a relatively small percentage of the U.S. population engages in end-of-life planning, and that many in that group simply designate a trusted relative or friend to make future treatment decisions, choosing not to issue specific instructions on future care" (Dresser 1995, 34). That's clearly not the case for Edmund, as he has an advance treatment directive as well as a proxy decision maker, but Dresser also worries that in drawing up an advance directive, competent patients might not be very well informed about the physical states they may one day find themselves in, and they may not understand the meaning or implications of their decisions.

Most important, for our purposes, she worries that "the rigid adherence to advance planning Dworkin endorses leaves no room for the changes of heart that can lead us to deviate from our earlier choices. All of us are familiar with decisions we have later come to recognize as ill suited to our subsequent situations" (35). So it's probably not fair to say that Dresser favors the sovereignty of Patient-Edmund—it's more that she would remind us, and rightly, that Tosca-Edmund is a moving target who changes in sometimes dramatic respects over the course of his lifetime. He *is* Patient-Edmund, with the long history of Tosca-Edmund behind him. And he might have changed his mind about the importance of things that mattered to him before he became seriously ill: dying at home, dying naturally, dying without "extraordinary means."

While Dresser is right to point out that people sometimes change their minds, it doesn't follow that most of us want professional caregivers to make decisions for us when we're too ill to make our wishes known. Arguably, that's why some of us execute advance directives in the first place. And even those who have no directives seem to want their treatment decisions to be made by someone other than their doctors. The gerontologist and bioethicist Joanne Lynn writes, "I have had a number of seriously ill patients say that their next of kin will attend to some choice if it comes up. When challenged with the possibility that the next of kin might decide in a way that was not what the patient would have chosen, the patient would kindly calm my concern with the observation that such an error would not be very important" (Lynn 1991, 103). According to a recent study published in the *American Journal of Respiratory and Critical Care Medicine*, even the majority of proxy decision makers prefer to retain control over value-laden decisions concerning end-of-life care, rather than ceding that power to physicians (Johnson et al., 2011). By appointing Charlie as his proxy, Edmund seems to have done his best not to cede that power either.

So, should Edmund be waked? I honestly can't say. My own intuition is that it would be cruel to subject him to the fear and other forms of suffering that would surely accompany his arousal, but that may be because I know how this story ended: when the man I've been calling Edmund was wakened, he was too ill to communicate his wishes, and he died a few hours later. That, however, is no argument; it's an anecdote, and while I've tried to motivate the thought that Charlie is trying, at Edmund's explicit request, to look after his critical interests, I haven't made the case that he should do so even though Edmund might be competent to turn away from those interests and espouse new ones instead.

It seems to me, however, that Charlie is probably right to want Edmund to be allowed to die without further treatment. After all, changing one's mind is not simply a matter of wanting everything done whereas before one wanted minimal treatment. As we saw earlier in the case of the Swedish vegetarian, it also involves an act of second-order volition—here, a repudiation of his desire to avoid a wild death. Possibly if Edmund were wakened, he would say that on reflection, such a death no longer seems unworthy, but up to now he's given no indication of it, and he's been Patient-Edmund for several weeks. In any case, the change-of-mind possibility can only be taken so far. Suppose Edmund were wakened and said he hadn't changed his mind—should Dr. Stoddard drag his feet in case Edmund changes his mind tomorrow? Next week? Next month?

On my analysis, among the many tasks that a patient might have appointed a proxy to perform, one is holding onto the patient as the person they have known and cared about, making decisions that reflect *that* understanding of who the patient is. Presumably, it has mattered to the patient that his prehospitalization identity be maintained, since otherwise it's hard to see why he would have appointed a proxy in the first place. It can't be solely because he wants his experiential interests to be safeguarded, as those are the responsibility of the professional health care staff. And while it's true that prudence dictates having a family member or friend on hand to make sure the professionals are neither overzealous nor negligent in their care for the patient, that's not the proxy's primary duty. She is charged with making decisions, and even if the patient doesn't articulate it in so many words, he may have chosen her to do it or trusted her to do it because she is one of the people—perhaps the most important person—who has been holding the patient in his identity all along.

Holding, as we have seen, doesn't kick in just in case the patient is permanently incapable of exercising his own autonomy, which is when, under the law, the proxy is empowered to make decisions for the patient. Holding has usually been going on for years, and it can be a matter of great moral importance to patient and proxy alike that the proxy makes sure it continues to go on to the very end of the patient's life. It might not be of the highest importance, of course. There are times when it's more important that a particular patient be treated kindly, that an unresponsive medical bureaucracy be prodded into action, or, especially if the patient is poor or powerless, that his rights be vigilantly protected, all of which a proxy might be appointed to do.

Nor is all holding morally positive. As we've seen, there are many ways in which holding misfires morally, either through active ill will or passive lack of attention. It can also be badly done if the one doing the holding has a mistaken view of who the person is. But patient-designated proxies have some reason to think that the holding they do is wanted and welcome. If I am right about how holding works, the proxy designation could simply formalize an arrangement that has been a source of satisfaction to the patient for quite some time. The designation then expresses the patient's belief that *this* person knows how to hold him properly, and he would like him to keep on doing it.

Whether anything like this is what people consciously think about when they name a proxy decision maker is an open question. My guess is that they don't, because the practice of holding patients in their identities isn't one that gets talked about in the way I am doing here. I think, though, that the practice is instantly recognizable, and if patients were asked why they chose the proxies they did, their answers would reflect something of what I am describing.

DISAGREEMENTS WITHIN THE FAMILY

Now let's change the opening scenario a little. Suppose Charlie is not Edmund's friend but his son, and suppose Edmund also has a daughter, Charlotte. Suppose, too, that like most people, Edmund never executed an advance treatment directive or appointed a proxy decision maker. Now Charlie and Charlotte are both in Dr. Stoddard's office, and while Charlie still wants ventilator support removed immediately so that Edmund can die in the way Charlie believes he wanted to, Charlotte is vigorously opposed to this. She lives in another state, and while her job as an office manager makes it difficult for her to get time off to visit her father, she loves him very much and has managed to see him regularly four or five times a year. When Edmund was hospitalized three weeks ago, she moved heaven and earth to organize things at work so she could be with him and has visited him faithfully every day. Now, visibly distressed, she turns to her brother.

"Charlie, no!" she cries. "We can't just let him go. There's still a chance he'll pull through this—you heard what Dr. Stoddard said. You want to take that chance away from him? You *want* him to die? I thought you loved him!"

Charlie tries to reassure her and gives his reasons for thinking that their father wouldn't want to be kept alive in this way. Charlotte does her best to listen to what he's saying, but the conversation just goes round and round until Charlotte bursts into tears. Dr. Stoddard, clearly uncomfortable with this display of emotion, suggests that they move their conversation to the waiting room outside the cardiac care unit and let him know what they decide.

In a recent paper in the journal *Research on Aging*, two communications scholars reported the results of a careful study of conversations about the end of life between 121 elderly people and their adult children. They found that the conversationalists, all self-selected participants in the study, were engaged in several different and sometimes competing tasks: one was to ascertain the elderly persons' wishes concerning their care when they were no longer able to care for themselves, but another was to define or redefine the parent-child relationship, and a third was to engage in various kinds of identity-work. They concluded that

> part of the difficulty of discussing end-of-life choices arises from communication dilemmas in which pursuing certain interaction goals interferes with accomplishing other relevant goals, such as when the goal of knowing a family member's end-of-life preferences conflicts with the goal of not wanting to threaten the person's identity as an independent decision maker, or when the goal of affirming the relationship prevents family members from reaching a decision. (Scott and Caughlin 2012, 687–88)

As the authors point out, some of the conversational pairs may not feel the need to discuss end-of-life topics because they are already familiar with each others' wishes. Another possibility may be that certain parents see no point in making specific plans, preferring to trust that their child will make whatever decisions seem best when the time comes. But the study suggests that the complexity of the competing goals can make it difficult for people to engage in these conversations successfully.

While that study involved only parent-child dyads, its findings may be equally applicable to end-of-life conversations between adult siblings caring for an extremely ill parent. As brother and sister do their best to hold their father in his identity while making a treatment decision for him, they may also be trying to hold each other in their respective identities, while simultaneously trying to preserve their sibling relationship—and they're doing it within a hospital culture whose manners and mores are foreign to them, at a time when they are trying to deal with their own fears, hopes, grief, and sense of the enormity of the occasion. That's a lot to ask of any conversation. It's hardly surprising that Charlotte should burst into tears.

They need help, not merely conversational and emotional but also moral help. A hospital chaplain or clinical ethicist might be able to make some useful distinctions, such as the one between sustaining a life and contributing to a wild death, or the one between wanting something previously unwanted and changing your mind. Such a person might also help them "identify and navigate the competing goals that can arise in end-of-life decision making" (Scott and Coughlin 2012, 688) and perhaps as well encourage them to set priorities among those goals. At the end of the day, however, Charlie and Charlotte are left with a difficult decision, and then they do well to remember that there are good and bad ways to stop treatment, just as there are good and bad ways to continue it. Perhaps they will at least be able to hold each other in some good-enough fashion and so sustain their own relationship, whatever else they decide to do.

WHAT COUNTS AS ENOUGH AUTONOMY?

If bioethicists have done nothing else in the fifty years or so since their interdisciplinary field was first established, they've preached the moral necessity of respecting patients' autonomy. If patients are capable of deciding for themselves what medical treatments they want, or want to refuse, others may not override their decisions—not even decisions to stop life-sustaining treatment. But then the question arises as to how autonomous a patient must be for his choices to be respected.

In a recent paper, Agnieszka Jaworska considers the case of Mr. Lazaroff, a man in his early sixties who was dying of extensive and untreatable cancer. Some years ago, Lazaroff had seen his wife endure a long, slow death in intensive care on a ventilator, and since then he had often said to his son David that he didn't want anything like that to happen to him. Now, though, with only weeks to live, he was faced with just two options. One was to undergo palliative surgery that offered a last-ditch chance to keep his cancer-ravaged spinal cord from getting worse and possibly restore a little strength to his legs and sphincters. His odds of surviving the surgery were slim, and if he did get through it, he would face a long, difficult, and painful recovery. The other option was to go home and resume hospice care, where his immobility and incontinence would certainly worsen but where he could be kept comfortable and die peacefully.

Lazaroff could not accept that he was dying. Despite being told several times that the surgery wouldn't cure him and could in fact kill him, he was adamant about receiving every treatment that offered even a remote possibility of staving off death. "Don't you give up on me," he told David. "You give me every chance I've got." The operation was technically a success, but in its aftermath, Lazaroff developed many severe complications. Soon thereafter, he died exactly the way he hadn't wanted to die—"strapped down and sedated, tubes in every natural orifice and in several new ones, and on a ventilator" (Jaworska 2009, 81).

Atul Gawande, the physician who reported this case, suggested that a paternalistic intervention would have been appropriate here, as the patient's choice contradicted his professed values and so seems not to have been autonomous. Jaworska, however, argues that a person who chooses in favor of something he cares about that conflicts with his professed values may nevertheless be autonomous, albeit minimally autonomous. She claims that on the liberal view of respect for autonomy, which she seems to endorse, if Lazaroff's request for surgery is indeed an expression of minimal autonomy, he deserves the same high levels of protection against paternalism as persons with full autonomy. Were either David or his doctor paternalistically to force him to die more peacefully at home, they would be doing something seriously wrong.

I disagree. I argue that if minimally autonomous agents were once fully autonomous, the values they then professed and reflectively endorsed have a greater claim to respect than what they care about now. Particularly if their choice is self-destructive, those nearest to them can have role-related responsibilities to coerce them into acting in accordance with their reflectively endorsed values.

Let's take a closer look at Jaworska's argument. According to the liberal doctrine of respect for autonomy, she observes, the only reason to interfere with an autonomous agent's choice is that it harms a third party. "Choices that are problematic merely because they reflect shallow values, or harm only the chooser's own interests or dignity, need to be respected. On the standard liberal approach, each individual's *capacity* for autonomy is the ground of value and the most fundamental locus of respect" (Jaworska 2009, 83).

She acknowledges, of course, that someone with a capacity for autonomy could make a choice that isn't in fact autonomous. The person might be deceived, for example, or her capacity for autonomy might be temporarily disengaged because of weakness of will or poor means-ends reasoning. "Even those with strong liberal leanings," she remarks, "may be tempted to intervene when a person's decision does not seem to truly reflect the person's autonomous will" (Jaworska 2009, 85). Jaworska has no quarrel with that sort of intervention. Her claim is rather that even if we don't need to respect *every* choice an autonomous person makes, but only the choices that are in fact autonomous, there are more such choices than is generally assumed. "Some choices that initially may look problematic deserve not only basic respect as pro forma expressions of the chooser's capacity for autonomy but also full deference as choices that are indeed the agent's own" (88). In particular, she argues, a person who *cares* about something that conflicts with his values may choose in accordance with his caring and so against his values, yet still be choosing autonomously.

Jaworska's crucial distinction between caring and valuing hinges on assessment. Valuing, she argues, requires "reflexive understanding of one's own mental states—be it one's own motivations or the correctness of one's own beliefs" (Jaworska 2009, 93). One must be able to endorse one's belief in the worth of what one values, or at least one has to want to value what one values. Caring, by contrast, requires no endorsement of either belief or volition. It's an attitude that can be taken up by even very young children, who lack the cognition to form the judgments of correctness that are "necessary for the proper grasp of any evaluative concept" (91). Because children as young as two or three can care but can't form evaluative judgments, Jaworska concludes that caring "presupposes neither motivational hierarchy nor evaluation" (91).

She offers three minimal conditions of an autonomously made decision: (1) the attitude that guides the decision must properly represent the agent's self, (2) the agent governs herself by seeing reason to pursue what this attitude prescribes, and (3) the agent is capable of reflection that leaves her open to the possibility of seeing things otherwise than she does. "Actions grounded in caring," she claims, "can meet these conditions" (Jaworska 2009, 88).

Jaworska's first condition has to do with the "self" of self-governance. The attitude that guides the decision must be truly the agent's own, as it's only when an action stems from attitudes that properly express the self that it can be considered autonomous. In this sense, we can talk about an attitude's internality. Philosophical conceptions of internality take value judgments or second-order desires to be paradigmatic internal attitudes: the agent assesses a thing's goodness or badness or, in an act of self-reflection, she steps back from her ordinary first-order motivations and either evaluates them or assesses them by further desires, such as the desire that she not possess a particular desire. Jaworska argues, however, that neither value judgments nor second-order desires are needed for an attitude to be one's own. Caring—a nonhierarchical, nonevaluative attitude—truly represents the agent's self, so it meets the first condition for minimal autonomy.

The second condition moves us to the "governance" part of self-governance: the agent must truly *govern* himself by his choice of action. This means, says Jaworska, that he must treat the consideration on which he chooses to act as a reason in favor of the action. In this way she secures intentionality as well as internality. But, she argues, there need be nothing evaluative about intentionality either: the agent needn't regard being guided by the consideration as *correct*, or not being so guided as a *mistake*. Taking what one cares about as one's reason for acting, says Jaworska, "is sufficient for the governance aspect of autonomy, and evaluating or judging good need not be involved" (Jaworska 2009, 94). Caring therefore meets the second condition of minimal autonomy as well.

The third condition is mental freedom: the agent can't simply be in the grip of her reason for acting. Here Jaworska has in mind the emotions of fear, jealousy, or infatuation that can hijack a person's perceptions and trap her in a rigid point of view. What frees her, says Jaworska, is "some openness to the possibility of seeing things otherwise" (Jaworska 2009, 96), but again, no evaluative measures are required. Jaworska appeals to Gary Watson's notion of reflection as a first-order phenomenon: reflection needn't take the agent's own motivations as its object but can instead be a matter of considering "various courses of action and their consequences in one's particular circumstances" (97). As long as the agent is capable of entertaining alternatives to her own care-based reasons, she is not merely in the grip of caring and therefore meets the third condition for minimal autonomy.

Let me begin my criticism here, with this third condition. Because Jaworska thinks that choices based on care by their very nature fulfill the first two conditions (the attitude guiding the choice is the agent's own and she governs herself by her choice), she believes she requires the third condition, mental freedom, to head off the unwelcome outcome that caring three-year-olds are minimally autonomous: children of that age, she points out, are incapable of the reflection needed to gain an alternative perspective on the reasons that make sense to them at the moment. But the third condition doesn't block that unwelcome outcome at all. Children no more than three years old are perfectly capable of considering alternatives to their care-based reasons and changing their conduct accordingly: three-year-old Jack-Jack, recall, is perfectly capable of refraining from spitting in his milk when he sees that it makes his mother mad. Yet, like Jaworska, we don't want to say that three-year-olds are even minimally autonomous. It's not only permissible but sometimes morally incumbent on adults to intervene paternalistically to keep them from acting on their foolish choices, even if they *can* entertain alternative courses of action.

The first condition, internality, is necessary to any notion of autonomy, but it's worth considering what *kind* of caring we want to say is truly our own. Some of the things we care about are pretty trivial, as the spitting-in-the-milk example shows, while others—learning how to speak Spanish, perhaps, or owning one's own business—matter far more. Still others are so important to us that they enter into our identities: "I wouldn't be me," someone might say, "if I didn't care about my children, my religion, my patients." Or sometimes, my booze, my heroin. The objects of care that define us, whether we endorse them or not, would seem to have a greater claim on others' moral consideration than passing enthusiasms or sudden changes of heart, no matter how deeply they are felt. I'll return to this thought a little later.

What troubles me more than the internality condition is the second condition, intentionality. There is a sense, of course, in which even a two-year-old can be said to "govern" her actions. She is self-propelling; she has a certain amount of control over her limbs. To the extent that she can be said to choose to walk toward you when you kneel and hold out your arms, she might even be acting for a reason, although there's a real question as to whether her prelinguistic behavior is causal rather than responsive to reasons (McDowell 1996).

However that may be, what she can't do is govern her *conduct*—her general manner of comporting herself, her characteristic modes of behavior. Self-governance in this more robust sense requires both maturity and training. One must be old enough to understand long-range consequences, including others' likely reactions to one's proposed course of action. That in turn requires a sense of others as distinct from oneself, and a sense of oneself as nested in many complicated social relationships. And *that* requires the ability to grasp social and moral norms, along with a capacity for normative self-disclosure—the ability to reveal through your actions who you are as a person, in the light of others' normative assessments of you (Benson 1990, 55).

Three-year-old Jack-Jack, who meets all Jaworska's conditions for minimal autonomy, can choose to stop spitting in his milk because he also cares about not incurring his mother's wrath, and in that sense, he can be said to control his actions, but he's not yet old enough to reveal to others, through those actions, that he is gross, or disgusting, or hates his mother. Because he's so young, others' praise or blame of him will aim at positive or negative reinforcement, not moral assessment. They'll treat him as someone who needs to be looked after—someone who needs, in P.F. Strawson's slightly chilling phrase, "to be managed or handled or cured or trained" (Strawson 1962). They may not actually say to themselves, "This little kid lacks normative self-disclosure," but they will think he can't yet govern himself very well. And they will be right. The mental freedom required for self-governance, as opposed to mere control over individual acts, is beyond him until his prefrontal cortex—the part of the brain that plays "an important role in cognitive control, in the ability to orchestrate thought and action in accordance with internal goals"—is more fully developed (Miller and Cohen 2001, 167).

Once children possess enough of the requisite neural capabilities, the skills of autonomy competency, to borrow a term from Diana Teitjens Meyers (1991), are acquired much like other skills, by learning from those who possess them and then practicing what is learned. As a part of their training, children often need to be treated as if they already possessed autonomy competency because that's how they learn to *become* competent. This is one reason parents offer even very young children frequent opportunities to make choices in a safe context where whatever the child chooses won't harm him, but their training shouldn't be confused with the child's actually *being* minimally autonomous. And all of this is further complicated by the fact that children are continually growing, and gaining increasing levels of autonomy as they grow. Minimal autonomy, not in Jaworska's sense of mere caring without being in the grip of caring, but in the sense of possessing enough capacity for normative self-disclosure to actually govern one's conduct, might correctly describe a state that children with normal abilities begin to attain around the age of ten or twelve. It's not until the prefrontal cortex is reasonably well developed, by the late teens or early twenties, that people have the capacity for full autonomy.

Jaworska acknowledges that the "practical effect" of a minimally autonomous person's ability to genuinely exercise some form of autonomy is "likely to be masked," because the *expression* of a capacity for autonomy requires "vital supplemental powers." She names only two: "the ability to engage in means-ends reasoning (so as to be able to advance what one cares about in the concrete circumstances in which one is acting) and the psychological ability to convert one's decisions into actions (i.e., freedom from disorders of the will, such as addiction or extreme impulsiveness)" (Jaworska 2009, 99–100). Again, though, this move won't do. In the first place, it's not clear that one actually *has* a capacity for autonomy if it's so masked that one cannot express it. The ability to engage in means-ends reasoning and to follow through on one's decisions would seem to be essential to the ability to govern oneself, not "supplemental." And in the second place, three-year-olds can reason very nicely from means to many ends—"if I eat my carrots, then I can have a cookie"—and they can control any number of their impulses, but the ability to do these things doesn't qualify them for autonomy.

Because of the difficulties with Jaworska's three conditions and her corollary argument, I don't think her concept of minimal autonomy is actually any kind of autonomy at all. But let's suppose, just for the sake of argument, that she has characterized minimal autonomy correctly. Then the question remains as to why we should respect it by according choices made out of it the same degree of noninterference we owe to people's fully autonomous choices. The responsibility to shield children, for example, from the consequences of their more disastrous choices extends well beyond the age of twelve or so, when minimal competence is acquired. Indeed, the conflicts set up by the tension between the parents' responsibility to save their teenagers from themselves and that of permitting them the freedom to make mistakes are the ordinary stuff of family life. I have no wish to minimize the parents' duty of noninterference with many of an adolescent's autonomous choices, but I don't see why it should always take precedence over the duty to protect.

Matters are even more complicated in cases like Mr. Lazaroff's, where the person has for many years been fully autonomous, because then we must also consider the person's *critical* interests. This is where Lazaroff's son David comes in. If he and his father have been at all close, he would have a far better sense than Dr. Gawande where his father's critical interests lay and how big a role any of them played in his self-conception. Indeed, because David's initial worldview and earliest "thick" conception of the good were presumably given to him by his parents, a number of their critical interests are likely to overlap. However that may be, unless father and son are estranged, he and his father have spent a great many years interacting with each other on the basis of the identity-constituting narratives that set the contours of their relationship. And when either party to the relationship is in danger of losing sight of who they are, the relationship itself gives rise to a parental or filial obligation to care for the other by holding him in his identity.

We don't know enough of David's history with his father to judge with confidence what David's filial duties were, but here's a possibility: if their relationship has been good enough to give rise to a filial obligation of care, David may have had a role-related responsibility to recognize that the values Lazaroff endorsed while fully autonomous were more truly an expression of who he is than is his desperate caring to keep on living, and to intervene accordingly. If David had a duty to hold his father in his identity, he might have wronged him by doing nothing to stop him from dying as someone other than the man he has long been—from betraying, at the very end of his life, the values he explicitly and many times endorsed. Rather than let him self-destruct in that way, it's possible that David should have coerced him back into hospice care and a kinder death than the one he ultimately suffered. Let me explain, though, why I say "might" and "it's possible."

We are supposing, recall, that Lazaroff is minimally autonomous, but I have been arguing, contra Jaworska, that (a) her conception of minimal autonomy is no kind of autonomy at all, and (b) persons who actually are minimally autonomous don't deserve the same high levels of protection against paternalism as persons with full autonomy: they're more like teenagers whose parents must sometimes step in to save them from the consequences of a self-destructive choice. But this raises a question as to whether the notion of holding someone in his identity plays any real role here. It's one thing for David to act like the parent of a teenager, intervening to keep his father from hurting himself through risky last-ditch treatments. It's quite another for him to tend to his father's critical interests by holding him in his identity. Doesn't the duty to protect do all the work that needs doing?

To see why it might, let's stand the Lazaroff story on its head and imagine that Lazaroff had been a firm believer in the lifesaving power of medicine, telling David on several occasions that if he were ever in danger of dying he would want "everything done." Now imagine that as he lies dying, he steps out of character, as it were, and cares desperately that he not have to suffer any more medical treatments aimed at prolonging his life. He longs instead for a peaceful death.

Would it then be David's duty to respect his critical interests by forcing him to live as long as he can, despite the suffering it costs him?

Possibly not. David's duty to protect him from further suffering might outweigh any duty he had to hold him in his identity. But I want to suggest that it would depend on *how strong a critical interest* Lazaroff had in preserving his life. If his father's firm belief in medicine's healing power had entered into his identity only peripherally—for example, if Lazaroff were a black man who had by racism been denied access to health care for most of his life and was determined to get all the goods that medicine had to offer him, but now has changed his mind—then David does nothing wrong by allowing his father to stop treatment: nothing much is lost and a good deal is gained if his father no longer has to suffer. On the other hand, if Lazaroff had always been an observant Orthodox Jew who believed that God commanded his people to uphold the sanctity of human life, it would seem disrespectful of David to make a mockery of one of his father's most deeply held, lifelong commitments by letting him stop rather than forcing him to continue. It's worth pointing out that suffering is valuable or worthless exactly according to what it buys us, and if it now keeps Lazaroff from betraying an identity-constituting religious duty, David ought arguably to hold him to it. This is what I meant earlier, when I said that some objects of care matter more to us than others: the ones that are so important that they enter deeply into our identities would seem to have a stronger claim on others' moral consideration.

My argument here is a fairly modest one: I only want to motivate the thought that dying in accordance with one's reflectively endorsed values can be too big a task for a person to perform on his own. If he is no longer fully autonomous, he may need the help of others who love him enough to force him to do what he himself thinks is right.

In closing, let me consider an objection to this entire line of argument. A simpler explanation for what Mr. Lazaroff was doing when he opted for surgery is that he was *fully* autonomous and merely changed his mind. The default assumption, after all, is that people are autonomous until clearly shown to be otherwise, and that's as it should be—it's better to mistakenly respect someone's autonomy when they aren't in fact autonomous than to fail to respect autonomy when it's present. An autonomous change of mind in the face of imminent death is surely understandable, for, despite what people may say ahead of time about the manner of their dying, they have never done it before, and until it happens to them, they can't fully know what it would be like. Death is so—final. It is the end of everything there is, and that same everything might, *in extremis*, become tremendously important to hang on to for every moment one possibly can.

If Lazaroff really is autonomous, then David may not coerce him, though he is certainly permitted and might even have a responsibility to urge him strongly to reconsider. *In extremis*, after all, is not the optimal epistemic position for judging the importance of anything, much less of everything there is. It's the course of our life and what we have done with it that give it its final meaning, and while death-bed conversions are possible, they're a cheap substitute for having lived thoughtfully and lovingly all along. Here persuasion must take the place of coercion, but the motive is still the same: to hold this man in the identity he has borne all of his adult life.

When anyone suddenly changes his mind in the face of oft-professed views about something as important as how he wishes to die, especially when the person is extremely ill and the choice he has made is not only out of character but self-destructive, the default assumption shifts. The mere ability to utter a preference is no sign, in these circumstances, that the patient is fully autonomous. I remind you, one last time, of our three-year-old Jack-Jack, who has plenty of preferences and no hesitation about voicing them, but requires continual paternalistic supervision. So, too, might the dying patient. Those whose lives are bound up with his may well wonder if a sudden change of mind is really autonomous, and they're entitled to conversations through which they satisfy themselves that his critical interests have genuinely altered in this way. If they aren't convinced that the change reflects something deeper than weakness of will born of fear or disordered thinking born of terminal illness, they must not stand idly by, doing nothing. Friends, it is said, don't let their friends drive drunk. Those who love us shouldn't let us betray ourselves at life's end, either.

Perhaps it's when we are dying that we need most to be held—even coercively held—in our identities, that others may ratify the goodness of our lives and being, and keep us in that goodness. The way he died doesn't negate all that came before in Lazaroff's life, but it casts a shadow over it: he didn't exit his life as well as he meant to. Of course, Lazaroff cared, and cared passionately, about staying alive. But while he couldn't have this thing that he cared about, he might at least have remained true to his own reflectively endorsed values. What a pity it would be if even more people in his situation were left to die as badly as he did, out of others' misplaced respect for their minimal autonomy.

THE DYING HOLDING THE LIVING

The advance treatment directive and power of attorney for health care are the legal ways of holding others to specific forms of recognition and response at the end of life, as they are the scripting and casting mechanism by which the dying performer sets the scene she wishes other performers to play out with her; her authority to direct the scene arises from the generally recognized right people have to determine how they are to be treated medically. Informal mechanisms that serve the same purpose include the person's conversations with family members about how he wishes the scene to go, asking for or refusing certain kinds of treatment, and extracting promises that those nearest and dearest will see to it that health care professionals (or they themselves) will do or refrain from doing certain things to or for him. These are ways in which the person signals how he wants to be held in his identity, and a great deal has been written about them, though not in the way I am writing here. On the other hand, almost nothing has been written about how dying people hold others in their identities, but that, too, is worth a closer look.

First, I might just point out that in asking others to hold her in certain ways, the dying person is also engaged in holding them in the ways she sees them. When she appoints a proxy decision maker, she recognizes that person either as someone who can be counted on to carry out her wishes or as the person she appointed because he is who he is. She recognizes the professionals who care for her as health care professionals and responds to them accordingly. She recognizes visitors and, perhaps through body language alone, shows that she's glad to see them or that she wants them to go away. In asking a friend for forgiveness or telling her son she loves him, she nurtures those relationships even as she prepares for their dissolution, and in that way, she holds these people, too, in their identities.

There are subtler means by which the dying hold the living, as well. The woman dying of heart disease who refuses to be cared for at home any longer because she doesn't want her daughter to have to take any more time off work holds her daughter in her job-related identity. The man ravaged by end-stage cancer who insists on minimal pain medication so he can be present to his family when they come to visit holds them in their identities, and in doing so, he maintains his own identity as father, grandfather, and husband. The asthmatic woman in home hospice care who leaves her bed one night to crawl in next to her husband holds him in his identity as her lover, spouse, and possibly best friend.

At the end of life, holding can misfire just as badly as at any other time. Lifelong homophobes don't usually start treating gay people with respect in their final days, nor can we count on racists to undergo a deathbed conversion. The woman who believes that people who don't share her faith are headed straight to hell, or who has always turned a blind eye to her son's brutality, will probably die as she has lived. The man who despises his next-door neighbor for his foreign ways isn't likely, now, to send peace offerings across the fence.

Then, too, a terminal illness can itself make holding others very difficult. Pain, fever, or what's been nicknamed ICU psychosis can interfere with a person's ability to see others properly, much less respond well to what she sees. If the dying person is immobilized due to injury, muscular or nerve degeneration, or dementia, she may not be able to respond to what others are expressing. Or the person might be so terrified of dying or so absorbed in her own illness that she's unable to serve as any kind of audience for others' self-expression. She may refuse to recognize that her close friends and family are suffering, too, or see them only in terms of what they can do for her.

THE DEAD HOLDING THE LIVING

Although the dead are no longer agents, what they did in their lives can hold the living in their identities in all sorts of ways. The legal mechanism for this is the last will and testament, which not only directs survivors as to the disposition of the deceased person's property but also serves powerfully as an indication of how the testator saw the various people to whom she left bequests. The uncle who leaves all his money to a favorite niece so she can start the business she's dreamed of for years holds the niece in the "entrepreneur" identity in a perfectly practical way. The mother who leaves her children specific items from among her personal possessions also holds them in their identities: she leaves the musical child her piano, the excellent chef her collection of cookbooks, and the outdoorsy child her camping gear as a mark of recognition that holds these children in some aspect of who they are.

The informal mechanisms by which the dead hold the living can be much subtler. Consider the Little League coach who taught a small boy about fairness and courage and how to be a kind, caring person at the same time as he was teaching him how to play ball. He believed in the boy and showed him in many little ways that he was somebody worth knowing, even though, perhaps, he was the only adult in the boy's life who saw him that way. Now, many years after the coach died, when the man who used to be that boy has trouble holding on to his own sense of who he is, the memory of the coach's recognition and response to that scrawny, lost kid helps him get a grip. Unless we're very unlucky, we have all had someone like that in our lives—perhaps a boss who initiated you into the mysteries of the corporate world and encouraged you to see yourself as a rising star, or a philosophy professor whose unshakable faith in your talent got you over the rough spots in graduate school. Maybe it was a grandmother who fostered in you a lifelong love of gardening or an elderly neighbor who was so good to you when you were a little girl that she taught you how to shape your own identity when, many years later, you became elderly yourself.

As is always the case with identity-work, the dead can hold well or badly. The Victorian father who writes his daughter out of his will lets go of her identity in a dramatic manner that leaves no doubt about how he saw her. His deed creates new stories of who she is with respect to her family that now enter not only her own self-conception but others' sense of her as well. Less dramatically, perhaps, the parent who plays favorites, leaving one child considerably more than the others though all the children could use the money, says something about her understanding of who her children are.

When someone you love treated you very badly during her lifetime—usually this would be a parent, spouse, stepparent, or grandparent—that person can be alive to you for years afterward, still "telling" you how useless or selfish or stupid you are. The grandfather who molested you when you were in your early teens can keep on making you feel as if you're fair game for any man's sexual pleasure long after he's dead. The mother who continually criticized you can make you feel unworthy even as you visit her grave. Time can heal the lesser wounds to your identity, as most of us are fortunate enough to be able to forgive the small, often unintentional slights we constantly inflict on each other, but the people who have been powerfully present to us, in childhood in particular, can continue to damage our identities even though they died long ago.

THE LIVING HOLDING THE DEAD

Although the dead can no longer be held in personhood in even the minimal way my family and I held the badly damaged baby with whom this book began, it's arguably still possible to hold them in their former identities. Here again, holding can't take the form of improvised coperformances based on mutual narrative recognition, but because the stories that once constituted the deceased person's identity did not die when she did, those who mourn her can employ those stories in many different practices of preservative love.

Formal practices include, of course, the funeral or memorial service, a ceremony that employs those stories as mourners honor the person's passing. Shiva, the seven-day period of mourning immediately following a Jewish burial, is aimed primarily at holding those closest to the deceased in their identities as they grieve, but it, too, employs stories of the more important acts, experiences, roles, relationships, commitments, and characteristics of the person who has died. Wakes, which take place between the death of the person and the time of the burial, serve many of the same preservative functions. Many religions mark the first anniversary of the person's death with a ceremony of hymns and prayers; those who attend the ceremony are likewise practicing a form of preservative love. Some remarkable people are beatified or even ultimately canonized after death: in this way entire branches of the Christian church, and not just individual believers, hold the person in her or his identity. When a prominent scholar dies, her colleagues commonly honor her by holding sessions at professional conferences devoted to papers commemorating her work; these are sometimes collected in published volumes as an expression of the esteem in which the deceased is held. And giving a charitable foundation, building, or park a deceased person's name is another way in which the living hold the dead in their identities.

Less formal practices of preservative love include biographies or histories employing stories that contribute to the dead person's identity, reminiscences among family members or close friends, blog posts and Facebook tributes, and remembering the person in one's prayers. We repeat Grandpa David's favorite saying, hand down the recipe for Great-Aunt Bessie's pound cake to our children, store blankets in Grandma Florence's hope chest. Sometimes stories of who the person was are taught in schools or handed down in the family from generation to generation—distorted, no doubt, by the passage of time, but still serving to preserve the person's identity in the memories of those who came after. And sometimes we hold the dead by returning on a regular basis to a place that we strongly associate with them, perhaps a gravesite, perhaps a family farm or cottage, perhaps the house where they grew up or spent some part of their lives.

Here, too, of course, holding can go badly wrong. The dead can be slandered and their reputations ruined. The plays of Shakespeare can be falsely attributed to the seventeenth Earl of Oxford. Corpses can be dishonored, especially in wartime, by being raped, mutilated, urinated on, or treated in other vile ways limited only by the human imagination. The Holocaust can be denied, thereby erasing the existence and dreadful suffering of millions of Jews, as well as Romani, gays and lesbians, Seventh-Day Adventists, and people with disabilities.

Less extreme forms of morally bad holding include not honoring the person's expressed wishes regarding the disposition of his body or property. The wicked lawyer who quashes a codicil for gain is the stuff of whodunits, but a more common real-life example is the family who refuses permission to harvest a loved one's organs for transplant, even though the newly deceased carried an organ donor card. Matters are morally trickier when the deceased left no explicit or formally executed wishes regarding her affairs. Ill will among surviving relatives regarding a valued painting or piece of furniture is all too common, with all parties claiming with moral certainty that "Mother (or Uncle Arjuna) *wanted* me to have it." And sometimes, those closest to the deceased do violence to the person's identity-constituting commitments, knowing full well the person wouldn't have wanted to have matters arranged as they arrange them. Ray Monk writes that when Ludwig Wittgenstein died, Malcolm Drury reminded Elizabeth Anscombe, Yorrick Smythies, and Ben Richards that Wittgenstein had approved of Leo Tolstoy's sending for a priest for his Russian Orthodox brother, despite his own rejection of the church. This prompted the others to give Wittgenstein a Roman Catholic burial, even though, as they knew, he didn't accept the doctrines of that religion (Monk 1991, 579–80). Arguably, in burying him as he did, his friends culpably let go of Wittgenstein's identity.

Must we hold the dead in memory? In *The Moral Demands of Memory*, Jeffrey Blustein offers three arguments, all expressivist, for the obligation to remember the dead—in particular the people we have loved. The first argument is the "rescue from insignificance view": we remember these people to express our belief "that their lives had a point not even death can reduce to insignificance" (Blustein 2008, 272–73). The second argument is the "enduring duties view." "Duties appropriate to the dear departed," he contends, "flow from or instantiate duties of love and honor, among others" (273). Third, he argues for the "reciprocity view": we remember the dead because we, too, hope to be remembered, and in desiring to be remembered, we express a "fidelity to the tradition of remembering" itself (280).

The second argument strikes me as a restatement of the question, not an answer to it: what we wanted to know is *why* holding the dead in their identities is a duty of love. As for the third argument, I'm not so certain as Blustein is that the "tradition of remembering" has any value in and of itself. Or at least, I'd want to say that whatever value the tradition possesses is heavily dependent on the value of what is remembered. Confederate Memorial Day, for example, memorializes a Southern Way of Life that was built on the backs of slaves, who took a rather different view from their owners of what that way of life was worth. There can be all sorts of good reasons, to be sure, for remembering the past, the formula for figuring out the circumference of a circle, or an appointment with the dentist, and it does seem as if there are reasons for remembering the dead. But again, what we wanted to know is what they are.

That leaves us with the first argument, which appears to be the strongest of the three. It does seem to me that we wrong those to whom we owe love and loyalty if we allow them to depart this life unmourned and unremembered. Death has destroyed their existence, and while they may have made things that have outlasted them—a garden, a software program, a poem, a scientific discovery, a piece of foreign policy—these things can no longer be seen as *theirs* if they themselves are not remembered. So far as we know for certain, the only thing of theirs that death cannot destroy is their identities. Only we can destroy those, by ceasing to hold them in our preservative love. To let go of their identities, then, is the final and fullest obliteration. However despicable they may have been in their lifetimes, none of us, I'd argue, has enough moral authority to consign them to that.

Chapter 7

What Does It All Mean?

Of those so close beside me, which are you? God bless the Ground!
I shall walk softly there, And learn by going where I have to go.
         —Theodore Roethke

Taken together, this book's many stories and examples of holding and letting go become a picture of a practice so natural to human beings that it has gone entirely unnoticed in most accounts of personal identity in the philosophical literature. I think, however, that the picture merits philosophical attention. It adds a dimension to ethics that can both deepen our understanding of morality and help us in making decisions about what we should do. And it reminds us of something many philosophers have found it all too easy to forget: the essentially interpersonal nature of being human.

It's a picture, first and foremost, of a social practice—perhaps the most fundamental social practice. Like all such practices, this one is governed by rules, and it has a point: to allow us to live well in the sphere of special moral consideration reserved for persons. Healthy specimens of our kind are inducted into personhood through the same social interactions by which we acquire our linguistic, rational, and moral agency. It's of the utmost importance that this be done, as we would otherwise be damaged, stunted, misshapen, unable—recall Kaspar Hauser—to live a human life.

To be *held* in personhood is to interact with other persons who recognize us as persons and respond accordingly. Much of this holding therefore has to do with the narratives we create or borrow from the common stock to make depictions of who a particular person is. These depictions are our personal identities; what they depict is the self, understood as the embodied locus of idiosyncratic causation and experience. Identities are the personae we perform in our dealings with others; they indicate how we are supposed to act and how we wish or expect to be treated. All persons have personal identities, even if they are incapable of contributing their own, first-person stories to the narrative tissue that represents them. But those who are capable of full participation in personhood act on the basis of the stories by which they understand who they are, the stories others use to make sense of who they are, and the stories they themselves contribute to others' identities.

Holding someone in personhood doesn't necessarily involve what I have been calling identity-work, as sometimes the simple recognition that someone *is* a person who is expressing a facet of her personality is enough to prompt a response. You're leaving the convenience store and an entering stranger smiles at you and says it's getting colder outside; he's holding you in personhood. Or the clerk doesn't even glance at you when she takes your money; she's letting you go. As one-time events, these exchanges neither make nor mar you, but if no clerk ever looked at you—say, you are Amish and your community has shunned you, or you are terribly disfigured and people are repulsed by you—the many little instances you might experience of being let go could make it very difficult to hold yourself in personhood.

While exchanges between strangers don't require much knowledge of who the parties are, note that even in the simple convenience store transaction, the actors bear the identities of clerk and customer. Other day-to-day interactions are more complicated, and it's here that identities play a larger role. It's not that people ever express the entirety of their identity. When, for example, you find your friend weeping in the kitchen, she's displaying how she feels, not performing all the personae that are aspects of who she is. But she is performing a particular persona in distress, and it's that to which you respond, drawing on your own sense of who you are in relation to her. The right way to respond might be to let go of the facet of her identity depicting her as a drama queen, or perhaps excellent holding would involve sitting her down in a quiet corner and asking her what's wrong. However you respond, you are answerable to the moral norms arising from your and her identities.

FILLING IN THE SKETCH

The picture of persons I've offered is really just the merest sketch of the interpersonal exchanges that let us be fully human. For one thing, I've said too little about the things aside from people that hold us in our identities. A piece of land, a house, a neighborhood, an office—these can all proclaim or remind us of who we are, so that if they are invaded or taken from us, we feel personally violated. The material objects that furnish these places can also play a role in maintaining our identities. Familiar routines are important as well, as are hobbies and (for some of us) scholarly interests. So are impersonal institutions such as banking and the stock market. When these things let us go—when, for example, a mortgage foreclosure forces us from the house we've lived in for the last thirty years—the blow to our identities can be devastating.

More also needs to be said about the ways we hold *ourselves* in, or let go of, various aspects of our identities. When you leave home for college or your first apartment, you can no longer make sense of yourself with the stories that depict you in the bosom of your family. When your wife divorces you, good letting go requires you to allow the stories of yourself as her spouse to drop out of your self-conception so that you can begin to forge newer, longer-lasting relationships. When you outgrow a passion, your penchant for dressing like a skinhead, or your tendency to find someone to blame when things go wrong, you must let go of the stories that depict you in those ways or you can't fully embrace the change to your identity. Drastic alterations to your body make the same demand: when you drop or gain a lot of weight, give birth, lose a limb, or just get old, you'll have to scuttle outdated self-depictions if you are to adapt yourself well to your new embodiment. And, of course, you can hold yourself badly, either because damaging master narratives that represent your social kind as morally subpar have infiltrated your consciousness or because of the many other ways in which the four moments of personhood can misfire.

How we hold others in their identities typically has some kind of effect on our own. Personal identities are so often *reciprocal*. Obvious examples include husband-wife, teacher-student, parent-child, doctor-patient, coworker, and friend. Think, though, of the less obvious examples. When the stories you use to identify dark-skinned people represent them as dirty, lazy, sneaky, and stupid, you are a racist, and while you are unlikely to see yourself that way, the identity is nevertheless properly yours. When you see most other people as fair game for whatever you want to do to them, you construct yourself as a bully—although here again, you aren't likely to view yourself in that light.

Similarly, when Charlotte and Charlie, each doing it differently, hold their father as he lies dying, they express something important about who Charlotte and Charlie are. They hold themselves and each other in their ongoing identities as loving daughter and son—but the way they do it gives those identities a deeper, richer dimension than they've had before. When the girl sitting on the stoop in the dawn begins to call her fetus into personhood, she simultaneously claims for herself the identity of a pregnant woman, moving herself ever closer to motherhood as she carries out the work of her pregnancy. Similarly, how Ellie and Jack-Jack's parents shape their children's moral identities says quite a lot about who Mama and Daddy are, morally speaking—as do Emily's actions as she tries to hold her demented father in his identity.

There's also much more to be said about preservative love. I want to reserve that term for the love that preserves people from harm—including the harm of being excluded from or cast out of personhood, or the wrong of being altogether forgotten after we die. The examples I've offered have all focused on holding, except for the cautionary tale of Kaspar Hauser that shows the morally disastrous consequences of letting go. I think, however, that letting go can also be an act of preservative love. I don't mean letting go of someone's life when the time has come for the person to die—that can be the most loving thing to do, but I don't think of it as *preservative* love. What I mean, rather, is letting go of stories that you have used to depict someone unfairly—the sort of thing Iris Murdoch has in mind when she offers the example of a mother who feels hostility toward her daughter-in-law. The mother dislikes the woman's accent and the way she dresses, sees her as vulgar, and believes her son has married beneath him. Time passes, and on giving "careful and just attention" to her daughter-in-law but also to herself, she acknowledges that she has been prejudiced, snobbish, and jealous. So she lets go of the old ways she's characterized her daughter-in-law, now finding her "not vulgar but refreshingly simple, not undignified but spontaneous, not noisy but gay, not tiresomely juvenile but delightfully youthful, and so on" (Murdoch 1970, 17–18). To let go of the stories that portrayed the daughter-in-law unjustly and replace them with kinder, more charitable stories is arguably an act of preservative love that changes something about who the mother-in-law is as well.

Preservative love also sometimes requires letting go so that we can participate minimally decently in the practice of personhood. Here I'm thinking of stories that depict someone as too crazy, too monstrously misshapen, or too evil to even be human. For the reasons I've already rehearsed, by merely existing, anyone capable of communicating her mental states places an imperatival demand on us to scuttle those stories and replace them with ones that let us identify her as a person—maybe not our favorite person, but a person all the same.

But what, it might be objected, of human beings who really *are* evil or violently insane—tyrants who foment genocide, torturers, the man who recently murdered twenty elementary school children and seven of their teachers? Must we obey the dictates of preservative love even toward the likes of them? Arguably, we must. If there's anything to be learned from the sorry track record of man's inhumanity to man, it's that we are a species quick to inflict horrific suffering on others of our kind out of what often seems to be a sincere conviction of the others' moral inferiority. These convictions are so regularly wrong, so regularly used in attempts to justify the inexcusable, that we ought never to form them. None of us can know everything about another human being, and we certainly can't operate on the assumption that our own motives are always morally pure. Fallible and imperfect as we all are, we simply aren't wise enough to make these kinds of judgments.

Finally, I want to emphasize how *inexplicit* holding and letting go generally are, perhaps because they come so naturally to us. In this respect, identity-work resembles Wittgenstein's observations about aesthetic judgments, where aesthetic adjectives play hardly any role at all—the phenomenon Lovibond also notes in conversations about moral matters. When everybody understands how to hold and when to let go, much of what is important can remain unspoken, because the conversation "proceeds against the background of an essentially shared evaluative environment" (Lovibond 2002, 42). In letting go of Joel's self-proclaimed identity as a victim of his father's indifference, Francine doesn't say, "Don't play the victimized son, Joel," she says, "You *asshole*, Joel—shut up!" When I held Carla in her identity as my playmate, I didn't say, "You are my playmate," I said, "You're not so heavy, are you, my baby?" And when the man in the black overcoat and top hat lets go of Kaspar Hauser's personhood, he says nothing at all—he just does it.

If holding and letting go are generally carried out inexplicitly, so, too, are *conversations* about holding and letting go. Just as conversations about right and wrong often proceed by talk of what one might do, or declaring that one couldn't possibly do something else, or pointing out how late the train might be, so, too, conversations about holding and letting go are couched in language far removed from the words I've been using for it. You and your friends are having drinks in a bar and they start talking in a very ignorant way about something that, as they know, lies squarely in your field of expertise. You don't like being ignored, so you protest, "What am I—chopped liver?" You watch Jason characteristically botch yet another job: "Yep, that's Jason." The cardiologist schedules a meeting with you and your husband to tell you that your grandmother is now experiencing multiple organ failure. After explaining this as gently as he can, he says, "It's time to rethink the goals of Ms. Sanchez's treatment."

Although descriptions of identity-work play hardly any role at all in how the work is actually done, it has seemed to me that this work is too important to be left altogether undescribed. As I began to write about it, though, I came to see how hard it was to find words to characterize it, and that is why I settled, in the main, for stories that depict various forms of the practice over the span of a lifetime. On continued reflection, I came to think that this might be the best method after all—to show, by means of many and varied examples, precisely what follows from the fact of our essentially social nature.

A FINAL THOUGHT

It may seem as if, in focusing so heavily on that social component of human selves, I have lost sight altogether of the equally important individual component. We are, after all, not only what our societies make of us. At least if we are mature and endowed with ordinary abilities, we can also defy our society's expectations and decide for ourselves how we want our lives to go.

I don't mean to underestimate that capacity for choice. It's just as vital to the human makeup as the social component is. Indeed, we can think of human selves as comprising two intertwined strands that are often in tension and even, in certain cultures and at certain times in history, become unbalanced because one strand takes ascendancy over the other. Call one strand "the given" and the other "the chosen."[1] "The given" consists of our first and much of our second natures, the age and society into which we were born, the relationships with which we were encumbered at birth, the identities others impose on us, our first and maybe second language, and

---

1. Here's another distinction I owe to James Lindemann Nelson.

morality itself. "The chosen" embraces our status as agents who choose freely and act on the basis of those choices and includes our ability to reason, our free will, our autonomy, and our capacity to reflectively endorse or repudiate the considerations that bear on what we do and what we think.

Other things being equal, a self-understanding that values both these strands is better equipped to permit each of them to serve as a check on the excesses of the other. Excessive choice produces what Samuel Scheffler has called voluntarism (Scheffler 1997, 191–95)— the fantasy that all our obligations are a function of our choices, that we are atomistic individuals unencumbered by relationships to others, in complete control of the matters for which we bear responsibility. Excessive givenness produces fatalism—the fantasy that breeds undue amounts of moral deference to authority, trivializes the importance of our critical faculty, and requires the oppressed to be content with their oppression.

To avoid either extreme, both strands must pull in harness, not only within human selves, but also in the societies populated by those selves. In the current era, we are deep in the throes of one extreme. Americans in particular place utmost value on autonomy and (among their philosophers, anyway) hyperrationality; the voluntaristic fantasy is strongly in the ascendant. My hope is that this book, through its account of persons who without other people could not be persons at all, might help in some small way to tip the balance slightly in the other direction.

REFERENCES

ABC News. 2001. "The Army's $1 Billion Video Game." http://abcnews.go.com/Technology/story?id=97303&page=2#.UDOWTUT4aAc. Accessed 21 August 2012.

Appiah, Kwame Anthony. 2007. *The Ethics of Identity*. Princeton, NJ: Princeton University Press.

Armstrong, Elizabeth. 2004. *Conceiving Risk, Bearing Responsibility: Fetal Alcohol Syndrome and the Diagnosis of Moral Disorder*. Baltimore: Johns Hopkins University Press.

Baier, Annette. 1985. "Theory and Reflective Practices." In *Postures of the Mind: Essays on Mind and Morals*. Minneapolis: University of Minnesota Press.

———. 1986. "Trust and Antitrust." *Ethics* 96 (2): 231–60.

Banks, Sarah, and Kirsten Nøhr, eds. 2012. "The Reluctant Vegan: The Case of an Older Man in a Swedish Care Home." In *Practicing Social Work Ethics around the World: Cases and Commentaries*. New York: Routledge.

Bates et al. 2008. "Do Elephants Show Empathy?" *Journal of Consciousness Studies* 15 (10–11): 204–25.

Bellinger, Martha Fletcher. 1927. *A Short History of the Drama*. New York: Henry Holt.

Benson, Paul. 1990. "Feminist Second Thoughts about Free Agency." *Hypatia* 5 (3): 47–64.

Bettcher, Talia Mae. 2007. "Evil Deceivers and Make-Believers: On Transphobic Violence and the Politics of Illusion." *Hypatia* 22 (3): 43–65.

Blustein, Jeffrey. 2008. *The Moral Demands of Memory*. Cambridge: Cambridge University Press.

Bratman, Michael. 1992. "Shared Cooperative Activity." *Philosophical Review* 101 (2): 327–41.

Butler, Judith. 1990. *Gender Trouble*. New York: Routledge.

Calef, Zach. 2002. "Double Standard in Rape?" *Iowa State Daily*, 24 October. Downloaded 2 October 2012 from Strangetalk http://strangetalk.net/view-topic.php?f=5&t=26505&start=0.

Callahan, Daniel. 1993. *The Troubled Dream of Life: Living with Mortality*. New York: Simon & Schuster.

Card, Claudia. 2005. *The Atrocity Paradigm: A Theory of Evil*. New York: Oxford University Press.

Cassell, Eric. 1982. "The Nature of Suffering and the Goals of Medicine." *New England Journal of Medicine* 306: 639–45.

Cavell, Stanley. 1961. "The Claim to Rationality." Unpublished dissertation, Harvard University.

———. 1969. *Must We Mean What We Say?* New York: Scribner.

Dancy, Jonathan. 1993. *Moral Reasons*. New York: Wiley-Blackwell.

Davenport, John J. 2012. *Narrative Identity, Autonomy, and Mortality: From Frankfurt and MacIntyre to Kierkegaard*. New York: Routledge.

Davidson, Donald. 1986. "A Coherence Theory of Truth and Knowledge." In *Truth and Interpretation: Perspectives on the Philosophy of Donald Davidson*. Oxford: Blackwell.

Dennett, Daniel. 1976. "Conditions of Personhood." In *The Identities of Persons*. Ed. Amélie O. Rorty. Berkeley and Los Angeles: University of California Press.

———. 1984. *Elbow Room*. Cambridge, MA: MIT Press.

Diamond, Cora. 1991a. "Eating Meat and Eating People." In *The Realistic Spirit: Wittgenstein, Philosophy, and the Mind*. Cambridge, MA: MIT Press.

———. 1991b. "The Importance of Being Human." In *Human Beings*. Ed. David Cockburn. Cambridge: Press Syndicate of the University of Cambridge.

Doris, John. 2002. *Lack of Character: Personality and Moral Behavior*. New York: Cambridge University Press.

Dresser, Rebecca. 1995. "Dworkin on Dementia: Elegant Theory, Questionable Policy. *Hastings Center Report* 25 (6): 32–38.

Duden, Barbara. 1993. *Disembodying Woman: Perspectives on Pregnancy and the Unborn*. Trans. L. Hoinacki. Cambridge, MA: Harvard University Press.

Dworkin, Gerald. 1970. "Acting Freely." *Nous* 4 (4): 367–83.

Dworkin, Ronald. 1993. *Life's Dominion: An Argument about Abortion, Euthanasia, and Individual Freedom*. New York: Alfred A. Knopf.

Elliott, Carl. 2001. "Attitudes, Souls, and Persons: Children with Severe Neurological Impairment." In *Slow Cures and Bad Philosophers: Essays on Wittgenstein, Medicine, and Bioethics*. Durham, NC: Duke University Press.

Engelhardt, H. Tristram. 1975. "Ethical Issues in Aiding the Death of Young Children." In *Beneficent Euthanasia*. Ed. Marvin Kohl. Buffalo: Prometheus Books.

Fivush, Robyn. 2008. Family Narratives Lab. www.psychology.emory.edu/cognition/fivush/lab/FivushLabWebsite/IndexFamRem.html.

Fivush, Robyn, and Katherine Nelson. 2004. "Culture and Language in the Emergence of Autobiographical Memory." *Cultural Science* 15 (9): 573–77.

Flew, Antony. 1968. "A Rational Animal." In *Brain and Mind*. Ed. J. R. Smythies. London: Routledge and Kegan Paul.

Frankfurt, Harry. 1988a. "Freedom of the Will and the Concept of a Person." In *The Importance of What We Care About*. Cambridge: Cambridge University Press.

———. 1988b. "The Importance of What We Care About." In *The Importance of What We Care About*. Cambridge: Cambridge University Press.

Fricker, Miranda. 2009. *Epistemic Injustice: Power and the Ethics of Knowing*. Oxford: Oxford University Press.

Gillett, Grant. 2002. "You Always Were a Bastard." *Hastings Center Report* 32 (6): 23–28.

Goffman, Erving. 1959. *The Presentation of Self in Everyday Life*. New York: Anchor.

Goodenough, Abby. 2005. "Schiavo Autopsy Says Brain, Withered, Was Untreatable." *New York Times*, 16 June.

Goodin, Robert. 1997. *Protecting the Vulnerable*. Chicago: University of Chicago Press.

Gopnik, Alison. 2009. *The Philosophical Baby: What Children's Minds Tell Us about Truth, Love, and the Meaning of Life*. New York: Farrar, Straus, & Giroux.

Guttmacher Institute. 2013. "Abortion Policy in the Absence of *Roe*" http://www.guttmacher.org/statecenter/spibs/spib_APAR.pdf . Accessed 18 June 2013.

Haslanger, Sally. 2003. "Social Construction: The 'Debunking' Project." In *Socializing Metaphysics*. Ed. Frederick Schmitt. Lanham, MD: Rowman and Littlefield.

Hegel, G.W.F. 1991. *Elements of the Philosophy of Right*. Ed. A. Wood and trans. H.B. Nisbet. Cambridge: Cambridge University Press.

Hobson, Peter. 2003. *The Cradle of Thought*. New York: Oxford University Press.

Jaworska, Agnieszka. 2009. "Caring, Minimal Autonomy, and the Limits of Liberalism." In *Naturalized Bioethics: Toward Responsible Knowing and Practice*. Ed. Hilde Lindemann, Marian Verkerk, and Margaret Urban Walker. New York: Cambridge University Press.

Johnson, S.K., C.A. Bautista, S.Y. Hong, L. Weissfeld, and D.B. White. 2011. "An Empirical Study of Surrogates' Preferred Level of Control over Value-Laden Life Support Decisions in Intensive Care Units." *American Journal of Respiratory and Critical Care Medicine* 183 (7): 915–21.

Kant, Immanuel. 1998. *Groundwork of the Metaphysics of Morals*. Ed. and trans. Mary Gregor. Cambridge: Cambridge University Press.

Kittay, Eva Feder. 1998. *Love's Labor: Essays on Women, Equality, and Dependency*. New York: Routledge.

Knobe, Joshua, and Shaun Nichols. 2008. *Experimental Philosophy*. New York: Oxford University Press.

Korsgaard, Christine. 1996. *The Sources of Normativity*. Cambridge: Cambridge University Press.

———. 2009. *Self-Constitution: Agency, Identity, and Integrity*. New York: Oxford University Press.

Kukla, Rebecca. 2005. *Mass Hysteria: Medicine, Culture, and Mothers' Bodies.* Lanham, MD: Rowman & Littlefield.

———. 2007. "Holding the Body of Another." *Symposium: Canadian Journal of Continental Philosophy* 11(2): 171–202.

Lakin, Matt. 2012. "Bistro by the Bijou Owner Boots, Bans State Sen. Stacey Campfield for AIDS Remarks." *Knoxville News Sentinel,* 30 January. www. knoxnews.com/news/2012/jan/30/bistro-at-the-bijou-owner-boots-bans-s tate-sen/. Accessed 30 August 2012.

Lance, Mark, and Margaret Little. 2004. "Defeasibility and the Normative Grasp of Context." *Erkenntnis* 61: 435–55.

Little, Margaret Olivia. 1999. "Abortion, Intimacy, and the Duty to Gestate." *Ethical Theory and Moral Practice* 2: 295–312.

———, and Coleen Macnamara. "Between the Optional and the Obligatory." Unpublished.

Lovibond, Sabina. 2002. *Ethical Formation.* Cambridge, MA: Harvard University Press.

Lyerly, Anne Drapkin, Lisa M. Mitchell, Elizabeth Mitchell Armstrong, Lisa H. Harris, Rebecca Kukla, Miriam Kuppermann, and Margaret Olivia Little. 2009. "Risk and the Pregnant Body." *Hastings Center Report* 39 (6): 34–42.

Lynn, Joanne. 1991. "Why I Don't Have a Living Will." *Journal of Law, Medicine, & Ethics* 19 (1–2): 101–4.

Marx, Karl. 1930. *Capital.* London: Dent.

McDowell, John. 1996. *Mind and World.* Cambridge, MA: Harvard University Press.

McKenna, Michael. 2012. *Conversation and Responsibility.* New York: Oxford University Press.

Meyers, Diana Tietjens. 1991. *Self, Society, and Personal Choice.* New York: Columbia University Press.

Miller, E.K., and J.D. Cohen. 2001. "An Integrative Theory of Prefrontal Cortex Function." *Annual Review of Neuroscience* 24: 167–202.

Minuchin, Salvador. 1974. *Families and Family Therapy.* Cambridge, MA: Harvard University Press.

Monk, Ray. 1991. *Ludwig Wittgenstein: The Duty of Genius.* New York: Penguin.

Murdoch, Iris. 1970. *The Sovereignty of Good.* London: Ark Paperbacks.

Musschenga, Albert. 2005. "Empirical Ethics, Context-Sensitivity, and Contextualism." *Journal of Medical Ethics* 30: 467–90.

Nagel, Thomas. 1972. "War and Massacre." *Philosophy and Public Affairs* 1: 123–44.

Neely, Wright. 1974. "Freedom and Desire." *Philosophical Review* 83 (1): 32–54.

Nelson, Hilde Lindemann. 2001. *Damaged Identities, Narrative Repair.* Ithaca, NY: Cornell University Press.

Nelson, James Lindemann. 2009. "Alzheimer's Disease and Socially Extended Mentation." *Metaphilosophy* 40 (3–4): 462–74.

Nelson, Katherine, and Robyn Fivush. 2004. "The Emergence of Autobiographical Memory: A Social Cultural Developmental Theory." *Psychological Review* 111 (2): 486–511.

Nisbett, Richard, and Lee Ross. 1980. "Judgmental Heuristics and Knowledge Structures." In *Human Inference: Strategies and Shortcomings of Social Judgment.* Englewood Cliffs, NJ: Prentice-Hall.

Nolan, Kathy. 1988. "Genug ist genug: A Fetus Is Not a Kidney." *Hastings Center Report* 18 (6): 13–19.

Peterson, Candida C., and Michael Siegal. 1995. "Deafness, Conversation, and Theory of Mind." *Journal of Child Psychology and Psychiatry* 36 (3): 459–74.

Putnam, Hilary. 1964. "Robots: Machines or Artificially Created Life?" *Journal of Philosophy* 61: 668–90.

Rawls, John. 1971. *A Theory of Justice.* Cambridge, MA: Harvard University Press.

Reddy, Vasudevi. 2008. *How Infants Know Minds.* Cambridge, MA: Harvard University Press.

Reiterman, Timothy, Jessica Garrison, and Christine Hanley. 2002. "Trying to Understand Eddie's Life—and Death." *Los Angeles Times,* 20 October.

Rorty, Amélie O. 1962. "Slaves and Machines." *Analysis* 22: 118–20.

Rothman, Barbara Katz. 1993. *The Tentative Pregnancy: How Amniocentesis Changes the Experience of Motherhood.* New York: Norton.

Rousseau, Jean-Jacques. [1762] 2003. *On the Social Contract.* Trans. G.D.H. Cole. Mineola, NY: Dover.

Ruddick, Sara. 1989. *Maternal Thinking: Toward a Politics of Peace.* Boston: Beacon.

Ruddick, William. 2000. "Ways to Limit Prenatal Testing." In *Prenatal Testing and Disability Rights.* Ed. Adrienne Asch and Erik Parens. Washington, DC: Georgetown University Press.

Schechtman, Marya. 1996. *The Constitution of Selves.* Ithaca, NY: Cornell University Press.

Scheffler, Samuel. 1997. "Relationships and Responsibilities." *Philosophy and Public Affairs* 26 (3): 189–209.

Scott, Alison M., and John P. Caughlin. 2012. "Managing Multiple Goals in Family Discourse about End-of-Life Health Decisions." *Research on Aging* 34: 670–91.

Scully, Jackie Leach. 2010. "Hidden Labor: Disabled/Nondisabled Encounters, Agency, and Autonomy." *International Journal of Feminist Approaches to Bioethics* 3 (2): 25–42.

Searle, John. 1997. *The Construction of Social Reality.* New York: Free Press.

Sellars, Wilfrid. 1956. "Empiricism and the Philosophy of Mind." In *Minnesota Studies in the Philosophy of Science.* Vol. 1. Ed. Herbert Feigl and Michael Scriven. Minneapolis: University of Minnesota Press.

———. 1966. "Fatalism and Determinism." In *Freedom and Determinism.* Ed. K. Lehrer. New York: Random House.

Shapiro, Tamar. 1999. "What Is a Child?" *Ethics* 109 (4): 715–38.

Signorile, Michaelangelo. 2012. "Martha Boggs, Tennessee Restaurant Owner Who Kicked Out Senator Stacey Campfield for Anti-Gay Remarks, Describes Encounter." *Huffington Post*. 31 January.

Singer, Peter. 1975. *Animal Liberation*. New York: Avon.

Strawson, Peter F. 1959. *Individuals*. London: Methuen.

———. 1962. "Freedom and Resentment." *Proceedings of the British Academy* 48: 1–25.

Sumner, Wayne L. 1981. *Abortion and Moral Theory*. Princeton, NJ: Princeton University Press.

Sveinsdóttir, Ásta. 2012. "The Social Construction of Human Kinds." *Hypatia* Early View, article first published online 16 September 2012. http://onlinelibrary.wiley.com.proxy1.cl.msu.edu/journal/10.1111/%28ISSN%291527-2001/early-view. Downloaded 28 November 2012.

Taylor, Charles. 1992. *Multiculturalism and "The Politics of Recognition."* With commentary by Amy Gutman, ed., Steven C. Rockefeller, Michael Walzer, and Susan Wolf. Princeton, NJ: Princeton University Press.

Thomson, Judith Jarvis. 1971. "A Defense of Abortion." *Philosophy & Public Affairs* 1 (1): 47–66.

Tomasello, Michael. 2001. *The Cultural Origins of Human Cognition*. Cambridge, MA: Harvard University Press.

Tooley, Michael. 1983. *Abortion and Infanticide*. New York: Oxford University Press.

Trumpener, Katie. 1995. "The Time of the Gypsies: A 'People without History' in the Narratives of the West." In *Identities*. Ed. Anthony Kwame Appiah and Henry Louis Gates Jr. Chicago: University of Chicago Press.

Veatch, Robert. 1973. "Generalization of Expertise: Scientific Expertise and Value Judgments." *Hastings Center Studies* 1 (2): 29–40.

———. 1997. "Who Should Manage Care? The Case for Patients." *Kennedy Institute of Ethics Journal* 7 (4): 391–401.

Verkerk, Marian. 2012. "Ethics of Care in Family and Health Care." Unpublished paper.

Walker, Margaret Urban. 1998. *Moral Understandings*. New York: Routledge.

———. 2003. "Naturalizing, Normativity, and Using What 'We' Know in Ethics." In *Moral Contexts*. Lanham, MD: Rowman & Littlefield.

Walzer, Michael. [1977] 2006. *Just and Unjust Wars: A Moral Argument with Historical Illustrations*, 4th ed. New York: Basic Books.

Watson, Gary. 1975. "Free Agency." *Journal of Philosophy* 72: 205–20.

Williams, Bernard. 1981. "Moral Luck." In *Moral Luck*. New York: Cambridge University Press.

Williams, Timothy. 2005. "Schiavo's Brain Was Severely Deteriorated, Autopsy Says. *New York Times*, 15 June.

Wittgenstein, Ludwig. [1958] 2001. *Philosophical Investigations*, 3rd ed. Trans. G.E.M. Anscombe. Malden, MA: Blackwell.

Woolf, Virginia. [1929] 2000. *A Room of One's Own*. London: Penguin.

INDEX